Just One

A JOURNEY OF PERSEVERANCE AND CONVICTION

Just One

A JOURNEY OF PERSEVERANCE AND CONVICTION

Nour Akhras, MD

Global Bookshelves International
Louisville, KY

Copyright © 2023 by Nour Akhras
Editorial Director: Janan Sarwar
Editor: Rumki Chowdhury
Cover Image: ©UNHCR/Ivor Prickett

All rights reserved. No part of this publication may be reproduced, distributed, or transmitted in any form or by any means without prior written permission.

Printed in the United States of America.

Global Bookshelves International
Louisville, KY 40222
www.GlobalBookshelves.com

To comment on this book, email globalbookshelves@gmail.com.

Publisher's Note: The author and the publisher have made every effort to ensure the accuracy and completeness of the information presented in this memoir. Some names and locations have been changed to protect identities. However, the author and the publisher cannot be held responsible for the continued currency of the information, any inadvertent errors, or the application of this information to practice. Therefore, the author and the publisher shall have no liability to any person or entity with regard to claims, loss, or damage caused or alleged to be caused, directly or indirectly, by the use of the information contained herein.

Just One: A Journey of Perseverance and Conviction / Nour Akhras. -- 1st ed.
ISBN 978-1-957242-04-0 (paperback)
ISBN 978-1-957242-08-8 (epub)

Dedication

This book is dedicated to the first refugee I ever learned about and whom I deeply love; peace and blessing be upon him.

Prologue

February 9, 2023

I am a pediatric infectious diseases physician, one of only 1,500 in the United States. During the last decade of my life, I have treated some of the sickest children in our country, from babies with brain infections to toddlers with bone infections to school-aged children with complicated cases of pneumonia to adolescents with tuberculosis. I am also in the midst of my parenting journey with a son on the brink of starting high school, a preschooler, and two children in between.

Over the last few years, I have witnessed the slow rise of right-wing extremism, which includes the disdain for refugees in my own country and Europe, accelerated by the election of former President Donald J. Trump.[1] Over the last decade, I witnessed what happens when one group of people dehumanizes another through countless interactions with Syrian refugees across the globe.

I started writing this book in March 2019. The COVID-19 pandemic tabled any progress for two years until I picked it back up at the end of 2022. A few nights ago, the world learned of a horrific pair of earthquakes that struck southern Turkey and northern Syria, regions where millions of internally-displaced Syrians and refugees live. Knowing that so many people have lost everything (again!...since so many of this population have already lost their homes more than once before this) compelled me to complete this project promptly to highlight the stories of these families.

This book was written with a mother's sense of urgency and a physician's ability to look past anyone's origin or belief system.

Contents

The Invitation 1
The Interrogation 9
The Initiation 27
Realizations 37
Trust 43
Refuge? 49
The Snipers 59
Following the Flock 67
They Won't Remember 73
The Defeat 83
The Surprise 87
Compartmentalization 97
The Other 107
The Military 115
The Misogyny 121
The Terror 129
The Discovery 137
The Return 141
The Little Secret 149
The Resistance 157
The Building Blocks 163
Just One 167
Acknowledgements 177
About the Author 182

CHAPTER ONE

The Invitation

Chicago, USA 2017

"Perhaps, we could cross the Red Sea by boat to make it to Yemen, or if we fly into Djibouti," I received a text message. *Perhaps.* It is late August of 2017, and this is our second attempt to get into Yemen on a medical mission amid war and what the UN has deemed the worst humanitarian crisis of our lifetime. I replied with a swimming emoji. I admire dreamers. I am too practical to be a dreamer, but when you are a dreamer, you make things happen that no one would have ever expected. I already knew that about Zaher Sahloul, a pulmonary and critical care physician and our medical mission team leader. After all, six years prior, I had traveled to Hatay, Turkey, with him, my husband, and two other physicians to provide medical aid to the first group of Syrian refugees who had fled to Turkey in September 2011. Back then, about 8,000 refugees had just arrived. Today, more than 6 million Syrian refugees are scattered worldwide. Another 6 million are internally displaced; over half of the population have been forced to leave their home and move around within their country's border.

Chicago, USA 2011

At the end of August 2011, I was visiting my family in Chicago from Ann Arbor with my two small children, aged two years old and ten months old. I had planned to stay for about a week as I had some scheduled time off from work. My husband was going to follow me on the weekend. My cousin, Suzanne, and her husband, Zaher, invited me to share a breaking-of-the-fast meal in Ramadan (the Muslim month of fasting from all food and beverages, yes, even water, from dawn to sunset). There were about a hundred guests.

They had rented out a banquet room at a local Persian restaurant. The pink sunset reflected off the golden accents of the chairs onto the pale mint green walls. The room was airy, and the white linen tablecloths were fresh. The succulent char-broiled filet mignon shish kabob melted in my mouth. The tangy, creamy, savory mashed and roasted eggplant with its irresistible smoky flavor mixed with lemon juice and garlic was the perfect side. Furthermore, a large gulp of ice water was the ideal way to quench my thirst after a fourteen-hour fast.

I love coffee, along with my favorite Middle-Eastern dessert, *knafeh*. *Knafeh* consists of baked, shredded, crunchy phyllo dough enveloping a mixture of melted, stretchy cheeses topped with sweetened syrup. As I was enjoying my dessert, Zaher saw me.

"Nour, how has your Ramadan been?" He asked.

"You know. Surviving. That's the only way to describe fasting with two small children at home," I joked. "How about yours?"

"It's good. Thank you. Actually, I am making travel plans with SAMS [the Syrian-American Medical Society]. I'm putting together a team of physicians to travel to the refugee camps in Turkey," Zaher explained. His hazel eyes lit up behind his wire-framed glasses.

"Oh, really?" I had not expected a medical mission to be the topic of conversation.

"Yeah, and we don't have a pediatrician. Could you come with us?" He asked.

I had never done anything like this before, but in my mind, I was ready to go. I did not even have to think twice about it. However, I did have these two tiny human beings who depended on me, and then, there was my job.

"When would the travel dates be?" I asked him.

"In eight days."

Eight days? There was no way I would be able to find someone to cover my week-long of being on service as the pediatric attending at a tertiary care hospital, leading and teaching a group of residents, I thought to myself, in eight days. Nevertheless, I was wrong.

I got home late that night from dinner, but the next day, I called my husband first thing in the morning.

"Hi, Sweetheart. How are you and the kids doing?" He answered, having seen my number on the caller ID.

"You know. Crazy."

We laughed because he knew what it was like to try to exist between the two-year-old trying to gain his independence which included new-onset tantrums and trying to save the crawler from her curiosity which frequently landed her in trouble.

"So, listen, I am calling to get your opinion on something. Last night, Zaher asked me to come on a medical mission to southern Turkey to the Syrian refugee camps," I started.

"Really? Who is going?"

"It would be me, him, and two other physicians from Michigan. Internal medicine physicians. I would be the only pediatrician." I explained.

"You should totally do it," He exclaimed. I could imagine him sitting in bed, his big black eyes shining with excitement, his black curly hair crowning his bearded face.

He has always supported me, so I was not surprised by his answer. However, I was surprised that he did not hesitate, given how young our children were. My husband, Amjad, has forever been an optimist. He believes there is a human being on the other side of any situation who can be convinced.

"Really? How about the kids?" I asked. I am the pragmatic one in the relationship.

"We'll figure it out."

"What do you mean, figure it out?"

"I don't know, Sweetheart. Your parents, my parents... I could take time off. When is the trip?"

"In eight days. I need you to bring my passport, scrubs, clothes, and stuff." I had not left my home in Ann Arbor with plans for an international trip. "I'm also on service that week. I don't think I'm gonna be able to change that."

"Just try. If you tell your boss you're going on a medical mission to a refugee camp, she will try to help you."

So that night, I wrote an email to my boss:

Dear Beth,

I hope you are well. I am scheduled to be on-service for the green team [the resident team] on September 1st, but I am emailing you to see if I can change my schedule. Last night, I was invited to be on a medical mission team to southern Turkey to provide medical relief to the first wave of Syrian refugees who crossed into Turkey. I would be the only pediatrician and female physician in the group. Since I am bilingual and of Syrian origin, I think I could be particularly instrumental on this trip. But I completely understand that a week is a short amount of time to find a backup. So, let me know. I would be gone for ten days.

Sincerely,

Nour

Twelve hours after I had hit "send," I received the reply:

Dear Nour,

That's amazing! Go. We will take care of it. Your work there is far more critical. We will find someone to cover for you.

Beth

In March 2011, protests erupted in Deraa, a city in southern Syria, demanding the release of political prisoners. The protests were met with deadly force as military officers shot at the protesters erupting in countrywide peaceful protests over the next few months. The demonstrations were continually met with excessive force that ignited violent unrest and eventually exploded into an all-out war with the inclusion of Russia and Iran on the side of the Syrian government and the Gulf states supporting what would subsequently become the Free Syrian Army. Ultimately, as in all other areas where there is a power vacuum, a group of thugs (also known as ISIS) infiltrated the country and added to the violence.

No one ever expected anything like this to ever happen in Syria. The president of Syria, Bashar Al-Assad, was interviewed by *The Wall Street Journal* in January 2011. They asked him if he thought the Arab Spring would reach Syria. The Arab Spring was a pro-democracy movement between 2010-2011 grounded in Tunisia and Egypt as citizens of the Middle-East and North Africa took to the streets to protest some of the area's most authoritarian governments[2]. President Al-Assad answered in the negative with complete confidence.

My uncle visited the States the month after that interview in February 2011. In his late 70s, he was a prominent obstetrician and gynecologist who, along with his wife of the same medical specialty, had opened a hospital in the central city of Homs. I was born at that hospital.

My uncle spent his entire life in Homs, excluding a few years of residency training in the United States.

"What do you think, *Khalo* [Arabic for Uncle]? Is the Arab Spring coming to Syria next?" I asked him.

"Impossible. The Syrian people know better," he replied.

He and the president turned out to be proven wrong.

As the protests continued, one particular non-violent activist named Ghiath Matar stood out, with his infectious smile and short black hair. Ghiath insisted on pursuing peaceful means. He wanted to offer the

Syrian military soldiers flowers and water bottles. Yet, he was arrested and tortured to death at twenty-six. His funeral was attended by then US ambassador to Syria, Robert Ford, among other foreign ambassadors. Ghiath's wife was pregnant with their first child at the time of his murder. She had a boy named, Ghiath, Jr.

A prolific documentary about Ghiath's life was entitled, "Little Gandhi." There is one clip etched in my brain. It was when one of Ghiath's friends talked about what it felt like the first time they stepped out onto the streets of Daraya (the city where he and Ghiath were from), chanting for freedom. His eyes lit up as he said, "It's like we were breathing for the first time."

The taste of freedom.

The thing about freedom is that once you taste it, you cannot untaste it. Furthermore, most people spend the rest of their lives pursuing that feeling of euphoria that only space can provide.

Over the next few months, hundreds of videos were uploaded to YouTube by Syrian protesters. They believed that if they showed the world everything that was being done to them, anyone would come to their rescue. I am sure that no other event in human history has been recorded as much as the Syrian uprising had been.

There were videos of peaceful protests, gruesome massacres, barrel bombs, secondary bombs (where the Syrian army threw bombs onto the rescue workers), chemical weapons attacks, and hospitals and ambulances' destruction. However, twelve years later, no one had come to the aid of the Syrian people.

That was how refugees from Jisr as-Shaghur, Syria, ended up in Hatay, Turkey and why I received that invitation to join my first medical mission.

If you had told me as a teenager that I would go on this journey, I would have never believed you. Not because I would have never been interested in it. On the contrary, I always dreamed that one day, I would work for an NGO (non-government organization) and travel to underdeveloped countries to serve in a medical capacity. Nevertheless, I would not have believed that my first mission would be when I was a mother of two very young children. "Mothers of young children did not do that sort of thing," I had told myself. At least, none of the other mothers I knew would jump at an opportunity to travel to the border of a war-torn country like Syria.

The reason everyone thought Syria was unlikely to follow in the footsteps of the Arab Spring was that the previous president of Syria, Hafez al-Assad, father to the current president (Syria is not a monarchy), ruled with an iron fist. A Syrian uprising in the late 1970s to early 1980s culminated in an attempt on al-Assad Sr.'s life. He responded by pummeling the city of Hama using helicopter gunships and bulldozers. Thousands of people were killed in Hama in 1982. Anyone affiliated with the Muslim Brotherhood (thought to be the ones orchestrating the assassination attempt) anywhere in Syria was arrested, tortured, or killed[3]. For decades, no one raised his head, much less his voice in protest. Most people avoided talking about politics.

"Shhh! The walls have ears!" My aunt, Hanan, whispered to my sister and me on our first trip back to Syria from the United States as teenagers when we dared to inquire about why the president's picture was plastered all over public buildings and stores. My sister and I had grown up in Chicago listening to Jay Leno and the "Saturday Night Live" cast making jokes about the president and Congress among most governmental or political authorities. We did not realize that in Syria, we could be hauled off to an interrogation room and beaten for simply wondering out loud how the president continued to be re-elected with over 90 percent of the votes for decades. No wonder our Syrian relatives were quick to hush us. My sister and I just shrugged. *Maybe, something was lost in translation?*

Just One 8

CHAPTER TWO

The Interrogation

No one old enough to remember Hama in 1982 talked about politics. But young people in their teens, twenties, and early thirties in 2011, did not experience that fear firsthand. Instead, they were exposed to ideas of democracy and free speech from around the world courtesy of the world wide web. When demonstrations broke out in 2011, young people joined.

Although I could not predict the turbulent civil war that erupted in Syria in 2011, I did get my taste of what that kind of fear felt like—fear of one's government, fear for one's safety, and the threat of losing one's freedom. During my first year of pediatric residency in 2003, the FBI came knocking on my parents' door, looking for me. I was living in downtown Chicago alone that year. Life was much different for Muslims in America after September 11, 2001 than when I was a medical student a couple of years before this incident.

Chicago, USA 2001

I was a third-year medical student just starting in-patient rotations on 9/11/2001. Like most Americans, I vividly remember the details of that day. I was completing pre-rounding on my internal medicine patients on the wards at Rush University Hospital, gathering vital signs and lab results, asking nurses about overnight events, and examining patients. I headed to the nurses' station, where we usually met the residents but stopped to see a large crowd gathering in front of the TV in the family lounge. I found Ben, the other student on the rotation, with me.

"What's going on? What's everybody watching?" I asked him.

I glanced up at the TV and saw the images of the first plane pummeling into the North Tower, smoke billowing out of the skyscraper as the newscaster reported, "A plane has just struck the World Trade Center." It was silent except for the newscaster's voice. No one stirred. We just stared in disbelief as the second plane hit the South Tower. By then, the senior resident, Sandra, a tall, commanding brunette, had come to find us.

"We are starting rounds. We may have to prepare for all hands on deck in the ER. There is talk of a plane headed to Chicago. Ben and Nour, you guys are dismissed. Go home. Stay safe. Check your email regarding tomorrow."

Neither of us moved because we were not sure we heard her correctly.

"You heard me. Go! The University administrators gave us these instructions."

I walked home to my apartment. Thankfully, my roommates were still home because only the medical student left the house before the sun rose.

"Hey! Why are you back so early?" my roommate, Suraya, a student at the Art Institute of Chicago, asked me.

I did not answer her as I frantically looked for the 6 x 4 inch black-and-white TV/radio contraption that we stored on the top shelf of the closet. All four of us roommates had agreed to a no-TV policy, but my mom insisted on giving me this hand-me-down.

"In case you get bored and want to watch something," she had said.

"What's going on?" Suraya asked again.

I took the little TV to the kitchen, and Angela, the only one with a real job, was making breakfast. Her sister, Kristen, was in the shower preparing for her classes.

"Two planes just struck the World Trade Center," I said as I plugged in the TV and pulled up the antenna.

"What?" Angela exclaimed.

We gathered around the small screen and watched the images in black and white.

"Oh, my God! This is unreal." I whispered.

We spent the rest of the morning going back and forth to the small television screen. No one went to their classes, and Angela called in and was told not to come in either, as the non-profit organization she had worked for closed for the day.

As reports came in, a Muslim group claimed responsibility for this attack. Suraya and I, both of whom wore a *hijab* (the headscarf Muslim women choose to wear in public as an act of faith), did not dare leave the apartment. We were not afraid because we were responsible in any way. We were Americans, after all! Instead, we were worried that because we were most visibly Muslim and the World Trade Center attackers had claimed to be Muslims, we would automatically be targeted because people constantly looked for someone to blame.

I called my mom to let her know I was safe and to check in on her.

"Please, Nour, don't leave your apartment," she begged. "I am not going anywhere either today."

"I can't *never* leave my apartment again," I replied.

"We'll see what tomorrow brings," she said.

Later that night, as we lay in our beds, I could not fall asleep. "Those poor people," I turned to Suraya, the street light shining onto her face. "Can you imagine being at your cubicle, minding your own business, when your whole building turns into an inferno?" My voice shook.

"I know," Suraya shook her head.

"Or worse, the people on the plane, knowing they will never get off," I continued.

"The worst is deciding whether you should jump out of a skyscraper," she quivered.

The American-Muslim community went into crisis mode after 9/11. Not only were we lumped in with Americans under attack by al-Qaeda

— nearly 60 Muslims died in the 9/11 attack — but we were also lumped in with al-Qaeda by our fellow Americans and became suspects. Hate crimes rose against Muslims and others who were mistaken for Muslims based merely on a head covering, beard, or skin tone, like the Sikhs. Fear about internment camps being set up for us like they were for Japanese-Americans during World War II spread like wildfire. Muslim women who wore hijab were told to stay at home or leave the house without their heads covered to reduce being targeted. Like everyone else, I was afraid, but I also had confidence in the diversity of my home, Chicago.

I returned to the hospital the next day in my hijab and tried to resume business as usual. However, I knew that from then on, I would no longer be viewed as just a medical student. I would be seen as one of *them.*

One of the consequences of being an American Muslim in the immediate post-9/11 era was that, somehow, my name ended up on some extra security travel list. I never found out how I became the lucky winner in this situation. Without fail, every time I landed back in the United States, I would get picked up by agents either at the door of the plane or when my passport was scanned. Security agents would walk with me to retrieve my luggage. The walk of shame, as I affectionately called it, because I knew what everyone else was thinking about me: *I wonder what she did.* That never happened to me before 9/11. The Customs and Border Patrol (CBP) agents would then ask me the same old questions:

Where did you go?

Purpose of your travel?

Whom did you see there?

Where did you stay?

Where do you live in Chicago?

What do you do?

I usually answered politely. I am naturally non-confrontational, and I knew I had nothing to hide. One time when coming home from Toronto, I got annoyed when asked what I did for a living. I replied to one of the agents, "The same thing I was doing a few months ago when your agents picked me up and asked the same questions. Don't you people document and read these things?"

Bad move. It is never a good idea to anger the Customs and Border Patrol agents. They just prolonged the agony. Instead of spending the typical two hours in CBP custody, I stayed four hours that time. After years of CBP hospitality, my name was removed from the so-called enhanced-security list.

Chicago, USA 2003

Although my parents were well-aware of my airport experiences, they were still shaken to their core when the FBI came knocking two years after 9/11. Two men in a black Lincoln Town Car pulled up to our house in a quiet subdivision and parked on the street. They walked up the long, red brick-paver driveway and rang the doorbell. It was the middle of the day, and my mom was not used to getting visitors then. She was busy cooking dinner.

"Who is it?" She asked from the speaker system.

"The FBI."

"Who?" She was not sure she had heard correctly.

"Ma'am, we are from the FBI. Can you please open up?"

She quickly grabbed a hijab and draped it over her head. Cracking the door open, she saw one of them displaying his badge.

"What's this about?"

"We are looking for Ms. Nour Akhras. Is she home?"

"Uh. No. What do you want from her?"

"We want to ask her some questions." One of the agents reiterated.

"About what?"

"They pertain to her only, Ma'am. When will she be home?"

"I don't know. She is a resident. She doesn't have set hours." My mother managed.

"Here's my card. Please have her call me when you see her. It is important." My mom took the card.

"Have a nice day, Ma'am."

With that, they left. My mom's knees were shaking, and she had to sit down on the staircase after she locked the door behind them.

My parents had lived through the fear of what it was like to live in Syria in the late 1970s. Secret intelligence agents pounded on their door and demanded an individual from the family, usually a young man. If they captured him, he was arrested, interrogated under torture, and sometimes released, but most times, not. Years passed on before he would be released. Often, the day of his arrest would be the last day his family ever saw him. Sometimes, they heard snippets of news about him when other prisoners were released and could relay a message.

My parents could describe in vivid detail nights like that, even decades after they had immigrated to the United States. Such details become seared in our memory, and they live as long as we do.

When she finally pulled herself together, my mom called my dad. They conferred and decided to call their lawyer.

I had no idea what was happening when my mom called me later that day on my way home from work. Residency was exhausting, especially during the first year. The year I started, new rules were instated that did not allow residency programs to let trainees work more than 80 hours a week. Before that year, there were no restrictions on resident work hours.

The first year of pediatric training was dedicated to teaching on the inpatient side. For many months, I spent every fourth night at the hospital, being paged throughout the night to admit new patients, change medication orders or check on existing patients. The next day was a half day, and then I could go home and sleep. It was like being perpetually jet-lagged. When my body had almost recovered from a night at the hospital, it was time to spend the night there again.

On the day the FBI visited my mother, I was surprised by her phone call as I was driving home to my apartment.

"Hi, Mama," I said into the phone, awakened from a daze.

"Nour, don't go to your apartment tonight."

"What?"

"Go spend the night at your uncle's house tonight," she said firmly.

"What? What are you talking about? What's going on?"

Her voice became sterner. "Just listen to me. Don't ask questions, and do what I am telling you!"

Many thoughts ran through my head after I hung up with my mom. Did my parents hear that my building burned down? Had my apartment been robbed?

As a resident, I usually had an overnight bag in my car ready for call nights. So, I drove to my uncle's home in the suburbs. I saw my dad's car in the driveway. My mom opened the door when I rang the doorbell. I inhaled the sweet scent of her familiar perfume when she embraced me.

"What's going on? Why are we here? Why can't I sleep at my place?"

My dad was pacing back and forth as my mom recalled the sequence of events that brought us to this moment.

Never in my wildest dreams did I imagine that the FBI would be looking for me. Me. A 26-year-old nerdy, skinny, extremely shy pediatric resident. I had never done anything illegal. I didn't drink. I never experimented with drugs. I have never picked up a weapon. I barely made enough money on my resident salary to cover my rent and living expenses. So, no money laundering. I had seen everything related to the FBI on my favorite show, *Law and Order*; none of that was remotely close to anything I had done. Had I perhaps missed an episode about overworked, sleep-deprived pediatric residents crossing state borders in a crime spree?

Later, I realized that my parents feared a repeat of the horrific scenarios they had experienced in Syria, where people were swept up from their homes in the middle of the night. No one could do anything about it. I was living alone in an apartment downtown at the time. In the Syria they had grown up in, phones were routinely tapped. They believed they could not give me any information over the phone, another remnant of living under an authoritarian regime that spied on its citizens.

Eventually, a date was set for my interrogation after my parents had contacted their lawyer, and he made the arrangements. I did not share with any of my co-residents what was happening, not even with my closest friend, Karen, who came from Guatemala to Chicago to do her pediatric residency. I was still well aware of a country's cultural and political climate continuing to recover from the worst terrorist attack on its soil. This attack killed 3,000 people in fifteen minutes, undertaken by people who claimed they shared my faith.

"Mr. Horowitz will meet you fifteen minutes before your appointment in front of FBI headquarters on Thursday," my mom told me. Horowitz was my parents' immigration lawyer.

"Okay. But what do I need a lawyer for?" I am still in shock that I am going to be interrogated by the FBI.

"We don't even know what they want with you. It's better to have the lawyer there."

"Okay," I drew out.

I tried mentally preparing myself for this interaction, but how does one prepare for the unknown? How was I supposed to get time off for this interview? I needed to request the chief residents. I wondered if I should call in sick. Besides the fact that lying goes against my internal moral code, I am not even a good liar. Ask my husband. My face changes colors. I stutter. I look away, or I laugh. I would be a horrible poker player. (Yes, that's right, I don't gamble either.)

What if I am just completely honest?

"Hi, guys. I need to take Thursday off."

"Why?"

"The FBI is interrogating me."

I imagined the thoughts that could have run through their heads. No, that is probably not the best way to get time off for this meeting, I told myself.

This is what I came up with instead:

I knocked on the chief residents' door, and only one of the chiefs, Sheila, was there.

"Hi, Sheila."

"Hey, Nour. How are you?" Sheila was generally chipper.

"I am good. Do you have a minute to talk?"

"Sure, come on in." She motioned me in with her hand.

I closed the door behind me. "I need to take next Thursday afternoon off. I can do my rounds in the NICU (neonatal intensive care unit) and get my work done before lunch, notes, and everything."

"Okay, sure, but why? Is everything okay?" Her face had a genuine look of concern.

"Yeah, I just have a personal matter I need to take care of with my lawyer."

"Uh...okay. Is this going to be something that affects your residency?"

"No. It won't." I felt my face becoming flushed because, of course, I did not know that for a fact. Mr. Horowitz nor I knew what the subject of the interrogation was going to be about, but I figured if it came down to something that was going to be long-term, I would deal with it later.

"Okay, just sign out your patients to your co-intern and let your attending know that we okayed your absence for the afternoon."

"Thanks, Sheila."

"You bet."

Phew. That was not as bad as I thought it was going to go. The next hurdle to tackle was: *what does one wear to an FBI interrogation?*

Should I go comfortably? Jeans and gym shoes?

I remembered what my dad had always taught me. When it matters, dress to impress. Be professional and dress like a doctor.

Got it. Luckily, I had a couple of black suits that I had just used for residency interviews, and that was what I decided to wear.

It had been a whole week since the FBI knocked on my parent's door. I would be lying if I said I could breeze through work that week. I was walking around with this big secret that threatened to end my life as I knew it, and I was too scared to tell anyone about it.

That Thursday, I managed to finish my work at the hospital quickly. My stomach was upset. Although I am generally relatively calm and collected, I cannot control what the rest of my body is doing. Listening to NPR on the drive to FBI headquarters, my heart was pounding, and my hands were sweaty. "A car bomb exploded, killing 100 worshippers inside a mosque in Najaf [Iraq]," the correspondent had reported.

I turned off the radio. I figured it was best to drive in silence.

What could the FBI possibly want with me? It wasn't like I was an ostrich with my head in the sand. I was aware that since 9/11, the word "Muslim" had become synonymous with "terrorist," and the FBI was cracking down on the Muslim community in America. Of course, terrorism-related activities did cross my mind as the potential subject of the interview. Nevertheless, as far as I knew, I did not know anyone involved in any of these activities. Maybe, I *did* know someone, and I did not realize it.

The one thing that never crossed my mind was that the subject of the questions would be me.

I parked my car and met Mr. Horowitz outside of the building. He had aged since I last saw him when I was a teenager. He was a short man with gray hair and Clark Kent glasses. He carried a brown leather briefcase and wore a gray pin-striped suit and polished black shoes.

"Hi, Mr. Horowitz."

"Hi, Nour. How're you feeling?"

"Nervous. What do they want with me?"

"I don't know. They wouldn't say. Just answer, honestly. You can confer with me if you are unsure of something, and I will step in if I think you should not answer a question."

"Okay."

We were escorted to a conference room surrounded by glass walls. I sat on one of the swivel chairs and apprehensively twisted back and forth until the agents arrived. There were two of them in dark suits, crisp white shirts, and dark ties. Crew cuts. Mid-thirties. Fit. They took turns asking me questions, playing good cop and bad cop, just like you see on TV.

"Good afternoon. Thank you for coming in to speak to us today, Doctor."

"Good afternoon." I managed a small smile. *You make it seem like it was a choice.* I didn't know if I had the right to refuse the interview.

"How old are you, Doctor?"

"Twenty-six."

"What do you do?"

"I am a pediatric resident."

"Where did you go to school?"

"The University of Chicago for undergrad and Rush for medical school." *You guys are the FBI. Don't you already have this information?*

I wondered why the FBI did not just show up at my apartment or workplace. Was I supposed to believe that the FBI did not know where I lived or worked? Or was showing up at my parents' home, people who fled to the United States seeking political asylum, a deliberate tactic to instill fear in me?

After the initial few introductory questions, the rest of the interview became a fact-finding mission about Muslim individuals and organizations I might have heard of. The FBI was using me as a litmus test to see who, if anyone, was radicalizing the American Muslim community. My answers came in two forms: "normal" or "never heard of them." In theory or the FBI's mission, there could have been a third answer: "radicalizing."

"What do you know about Hamza Yusuf?"

"He teaches at religious retreats called the *Rihla*," I replied.

"What does 'Rihla' mean?"

"Journey," I explained.

"What does he teach?"

"Perfecting your manners, being good to your parents, treating your neighbors well, pursuing education, advancing civilization. Normal." I answered.

"How about Umar Faruq Abdullah?"

"He is the resident scholar for the Nawawi Foundation. Ph.D. from the University of Chicago."

"What does he teach?" He asked.

"Same sort of thing. Purifying your heart from arrogance, greed, and other deadly sins. Pursuing education. Integration in society. Normal."

"How about the organization IMAN [Inner-city Muslim Action Network]?"

"I used to volunteer with them in college. Grass-roots organization. We were getting inner-city kids off the streets, off drugs, and out of gangs. Staying in school. Education leading to a better life. Normal."

"What do you know about the Mosque Foundation?

How about Islamic Foundation?"

And on and on and on for an hour. Mr. Horowitz remained silent.

When it became clear that the interrogation had less to do with me and more with what I knew about others, it was my turn to ask a question.

"Why am I being interrogated?" I asked.

"We can't disclose that information."

"You can't tell me what my crime is?" I pressed on.

"We can only tell you that we got a letter that prompted this interrogation."

"And what did the letter say?" I inquired.

"It said you were planning to go to Afghanistan on a suicide mission."

I had never lived through the fear of interrogation under torture. My father hardly spoke of what happened to him in Syria's prison system. But every Syrian knows what happens to people who end up in prison. Unlike my parents, who were petrified until I called them and told them the ordeal was over, I was just angry.

"Really? A suicide bomber? And who is this ultra-informed informant who passed along this great tip?" I asked. Suppose this was not such a severe and stressful encounter. In that case, I might have laughed out loud at the absurdity of the idea that I would go to Afghanistan on a deadly mission. *I mean, at least make something up that is a little plausible. Perhaps a country where I actually know people or can speak the language.*

"We can't tell you."

"You can't tell me?"

"Yes, we have to protect the anonymity of our source."

Really? And who can protect me from slanderous accusations?

"So, I don't get to confront my accuser?" I asked.

"No, sorry."

Oh okay. That seems just and fair.

"Well, if I were going to become a suicide bomber, I would have saved myself from the doom of medical school or, worse, a science degree from the University of Chicago, and I would have gone straight there, don't you think?"

As I said, I am generally non-confrontational. However, even I have a line that, if crossed, unleashes a fiery storm of sarcasm that one might not want to be the target of.

Silence.

Maybe, they believed me when I said that I had spent every last waking second of the previous eight years of my existence buried under biology, chemistry, anatomy, pathology, microbiology, and pharmacology books in the library. Alternatively, maybe, there was no real tip, and they had made it all up to justify their fact-finding mission. I tend to believe the latter. Over a decade later, a friend of mine from childhood, Assia Boundaoui, produced a documentary called, "The Feeling of Being Watched," in which she archives how the Muslim community in Bridgeview, IL, where I went to high school, was under FBI surveillance for over a decade. She uncovers thousands of documents, taking the FBI to court to compel them to make these records public.

The most hair-raising discovery Assia made was how many of us were affected by this surveillance. However, we did not know it because we were too scared to share our experiences, as if sharing them would make us more suspicious. The most revealing discovery she made was that after a decade of active surveillance that produced hundreds of thousands of documents and occupied hundreds of thousands of workforce hours, our tax dollars at work, there was not one indictment on terrorism or related charges. Not one.

I never heard from the FBI again.

Soon after I married, I was never singled out by CBP agents, even though I did not change my last name. My husband believes it is because he is my lucky charm (*classic*).

Perhaps the CBP just got sick of how boring my answers were. Maybe they finally believed I was no longer a threat, or there was some syncing of information between them and the FBI (*I doubt that*). Whatever it was, my days of enhanced security and interrogations, thankfully, ended.

Despite these experiences, though the incidents rattled me, I did not feel alienated.

Maybe, I am naive, but I believe killing a civilian is killing a civilian. It's wrong. There is no such thing as collateral damage. It is just immoral, unethical, and inappropriate. I don't know how I would address modern-day war, but that is why I am just a doctor. I don't have to think about these complex issues. I can still take a stance about protecting every single life. After all, that is what my profession is all about.

There is a verse in the Qur'an that I find myself returning to at various times throughout my life. "Whoever saves a life, it is as if he has saved all of humanity" (5:32). To me, that means every life is precious. Once you recognize that, your contributions will only propel humanity forward. And the contrary is also true. If you take a life in vain, it is as if you have destroyed all of humanity. If you can justify taking one life, what prevents you from taking multiple lives? Or everyone's life?

This principle of ends not justifying the means is what drew me to the writing of the great Russian author Fyodor Dostoevsky when I was in college. I remember re-reading the passage in *Brothers Karamazov*, where Ivan, the intellectual skeptical brother, posed a hypothetical situation to his more spiritual brother, Alyosha. Ivan asked Alyosha if he would agree to "building the edifice of human destiny with the object of making people happy in the end, of giving them peace and rest at last." To do that, one condition existed: Alyosha had to torture just one child. Alyosha, the protagonist, did not agree, and I agreed with him. Even at the end of this Syrian crisis (whenever it will end), if the Syrian people ever become free and can elect a government democratically, will it be worth the lives of the hundreds of thousands who were killed and the thousands of others who were maimed?

Chicago, USA 2011

In Syria in 2011, unlike my parent's generation, who had learned their lesson, most of the demonstrators were young people who had never tasted first-hand what the Assad government could do. One of the first cities to take up arms against the government's use of force was the city of Jisr ash-Shugur, and the people paid the price. In June 2011, troops and tanks moved in on the town to fight off those who took up arms, sending thousands of refugees fleeing into Turkey. We encountered those people eight days after that dinner in August 2011 when I was invited to participate in my first medical mission. After receiving my boss's email, I started preparing for the trip that forever changed my life.

"Maybe you should just come with me?" I asked my husband.

"Really?"

"Yeah. I think this trip will be hard, and if both of our parents are volunteering to take the kids, maybe we could leave one with each set of parents, so it isn't crazy for either set of grandparents. You know, divide and conquer." I shot him a knowing glance.

He nodded in agreement and emailed his work to schedule vacation days.

I believed I needed emotional support. Although I knew what the betrayal of having your government accusing you of being a national security threat felt like, I could not quite imagine what I was about to hear from Syrians whose government was trying to kill them. None of us on the team had ever done a medical mission. We did not have any contacts on the ground. We were going in blind, but all knew that we wanted to help in any capacity.

My husband and I had never left our children for that length of time before. We had never simultaneously traveled and left our children in the care of others. As we were going to the airport, I tried not to cry when hugging the kids goodbye. All the parenting books say that when first leaving a child at daycare, make a swift goodbye, to not linger nor hesitate. Instead, we should consider giving them a quick hug, kiss goodbye, and let them know when you will return to get them. This was not a daycare drop-off, but I could not let either child sense any hesitation or worry. Although I probably hugged them a little longer than usual, I tried to make it seem as normal as possible. I left my ten-month-old daughter with my parents and my two-year-old son with my in-laws and set off with my husband on the journey that would alter the trajectory of my life. We had no idea what was in store for us.

Just One 26

CHAPTER THREE

The Initiation

Hatay, Turkey 2011

I have a very sensitive GI (gastrointestinal) system. That is one of the first personal facts I told my husband about myself when we first met. I always get sick when I travel internationally. So not 24 hours into our trip to Turkey, I spent most of the night and some of the morning in the bathroom. I remained unwell intermittently for the rest of the journey, so much so that one of the other physicians had told his wife upon our return that he thought I might be pregnant. His wife sent me a congratulatory message when we got home. How crazy, I thought. Who goes on a medical mission while pregnant?

"Maybe you should just sit this first day out. You are probably dehydrated," my husband offered.

"No way! We only have a few days here. We left the kids for the first time. I will get out there and do what we came here to do!"

On our arrival to Turkey, before we set out to the camps, we met a Syrian-American pediatrician, Dr. Zakaria, based in Florida. He gave us a lot of detailed information and much-needed advice. There were 8,000 Syrian refugees divided into five camps; sixty percent of the refugees were children. Dr. Zakaria was an older gentleman in his late fifties with salt-and-pepper hair and silver-wired glasses. He had worked in other refugee camps in the past.

"These are the cleanest refugee camps I have ever entered. They even installed washing machines in the bathroom facilities for the refugees to use," he reported. In addition to the washing machines, the Turkish government delivered three hot meals and two tons of baby formula daily.

Dr. Zakaria gave us a synopsis of all the common cases he had been seeing. "Many children and adults present with psychosomatic complaints, abdominal pain, and chest pain without any organic cause. Who can blame them after all the trauma they have experienced?"

"What are you doing for the kids?" I asked in preparation.

"Reassuring the parents. They need mental health counseling, which is just not available right now."

The blazing eastern European sun was beating down on my face as I stepped out of the faded yellow taxicab that had brought us to Reyhanli camp. The barbed wire fencing encompassed the perimeter of the sea of white canvas tents. At the entrance stood hefty unwavering Turkish soldiers, Kalashnikovs in hand, red berets tilted on stern faces staring us down. The first sound I heard was familiar, the wailing of a newborn baby, probably needing to be fed. Familiar but jarring, given my present location.

"Hi. We are with the American medical team." I smiled as I handed over our passports. No reciprocation. The soldier walked off, our passports in hand, to confer with his team. I peered in and saw rows upon rows of 8 x 8-foot tents, smaller than my toddler's room back home. These were the new living quarters for families of up to six people for the next few months to years.

"There will be an American pediatrician who speaks Arabic ready to see any of your sick children in the central tent. Please bring your sick children to be treated." An announcement was made over the loudspeaker in the camp.

I walked down the dirt road leading up to the refugee camp's central gathering area, a large concrete block with no walls and a corrugated white aluminum roof. The roof provided shade to those taking refuge from the sun. I saw a four-year-old boy with curly blonde hair in ragged jeans, barefoot, jumping in a dirty puddle. In one corner of the camp, a middle-aged woman wearing flip-flops and a green hijab messily strewn over her head was stirring a stew over a fire. This fire would, no doubt, become a source of burn injuries.

Hundreds of women and children surrounded me. I felt claustrophobic. There was no patient room, no examining table, nor any equipment. All I had was my loyal stethoscope, the blue one, which had been my trusted companion for many years, and an otoscope. So much for HIPAA (Health Insurance Portability and Accountability Act).

The first patient I saw was 14-year-old Amal. Her face was expressionless, but I immediately noticed her pale conjunctivae, a sign of anemia. Not to mention, her chief complaint was fever.

"How long has she had the fever?" I asked her mother.

"Two days now," her mom replied.

"Any cough or runny nose?"

"No, not really."

"Vomiting or diarrhea?" I inquired.

"No. But she doesn't really have an appetite," her mom added.

"Is she complaining about anything else? Anything that is hurting her?" I asked.

"She hasn't said anything."

Fever without any other symptoms could still be viral, I thought, and since that is the most common diagnosis, perhaps that is all that it is. But her pale conjunctivae continued bothering me.

I turned to Amal. "Is anything hurting you, Honey?"

"No."

"Okay, I am going to examine you, then."

She nodded.

Thankfully, one of the camp leaders brought over a folding table I could use as an examining table.

When I put my stethoscope up to her heart, it was racing. Perhaps, she was nervous or scared, but more than likely, this was her heart's way of compensating for the anemia. Her heart beat faster to pump the oxygenated blood to her vital organs.

"Has Amal ever had any medical problems?" I turned back to her mother.

"She had leukemia when she was ten, but we treated her, and she went into remission two years ago."

If a patient like Amal showed up at the urgent care I used to work at in Ann Arbor, I would have sent her for labs immediately. However, we were a long way away from Ann Arbor.

"I think she needs blood work," I told Amal's mom.

Her mom looked concerned. "Why? What's wrong with her?"

With her history and her anemia, this could undoubtedly be a relapse. Of course, I did not know that for a fact. But should I tell her mom? I wondered.

I face some of these same dilemmas in the United States. When I suspect a child might have cancer, that is not the first thing that comes out of my mouth when discussing it with the parents. I try to gauge the parents' reliability, level of emotion, and ability to understand. I go through many algorithms in my head in those first five minutes of the encounter. Ultimately, suppose I don't believe that the parents will take my request to take their child to get more testing done seriously. In that case, I do drop the C word. But if I believe they will take my advice, I usually say, "I think some more testing needs to be done to clarify what is going on."

I sent Amal to the hospital. I could not stop thinking about her for the rest of the trip.

It is hard to imagine this scenario. Here was a young teenager who had survived a potentially deadly disease. She had been ripped away from her home because of violence she did not even understand. She had walked hundreds of miles to cross into another country she had never been to and whose language she did not speak. Her new home was a refugee camp. And then, her cancer had relapsed.

It was difficult for me to make sense of Amal's circumstances.

That first day, I saw about sixty patients in five hours. Of course, as a pediatrician, I saw many children with upper respiratory tract infections, gastroenteritis, some cases of scabies, conjunctivitis, otitis media, and asthma exacerbations. I saw many women with urinary tract infections.

Many women were requesting OB/GYN (Obstetrics/Gynecology) services that I could not provide, and I felt terrible about that. There were also many pregnant women I could not help because I lacked the necessary training of an obstetrician.

I felt overwhelmed. Not only because I was not feeling well and blisteringly hot, but also because I was seeing patients in the middle of an open, common area, which felt intrusive. Even though they were children. Still. They should have the right to dignity and privacy so that the other 7,999 refugees do not have to see their exposed bodies. I tried my best not to undress them, especially if they were older or unnecessary. Still, every good pediatrician knows that a complete physical exam only occurs when the child is undressed. A comprehensive physical exam allows a pediatrician also to discover healing bruises, a sign of potential child abuse. I would fail if I could not rescue a child from such a situation.

The next day, I was thankful that I was given a private room to meet each child and their parents. I was more in control and developed a system for seeing and organizing the patients. Seeing patients in a separate room allowed me more time and space (emotionally and physically) to talk individually to the parents and ask them about how they got there or why they were in Turkey. However, I was not prepared to hear any of it.

For example, a middle-aged man named Ahmed came in with his three children, aged nine, seven, and five. He had been pushing his wife in a wheelchair.

"How did you and your family come to be here?" I asked.

"We walked. All the way from Hama." I googled the distance later in my hotel room. One hundred twenty-five miles was forty hours of walking without stopping to rest, eat, use the bathroom, or sleep. As veteran road trippers with our children, my husband and I always knew to multiply the driving time by 1.5 times to account for the number of times our children would request to go to the bathroom, even when we stopped for one at a time. I tried to imagine what it would be like to take a walking trip, carrying everything we could and helping the children and a disabled spouse for about 60-70 hours—walking for a whole week in rugged terrain in a foreign country where I did not speak the language. What circumstances would compel one to go on this arduous journey? I asked myself.

Another example of the stories I heard was a young couple, Maaria and Mazen, who came to see me for their three-year-old son, Mahdi. He had bright blue eyes, chestnut hair, and a mischievous smile. Maaria was eight months pregnant.

"Are you planning to return home once things settle in Jisr as-Shughoor?" I asked her.

"What home? The government destroyed our home." Mazen showed me a picture of a destroyed three-story building on his cell phone.

"The neighbors sent us this picture after we arrived here," Maaria told me.

Many families spoke of how Syrian security forces had burned down or vandalized their homes. *Syrian security forces. What a misnomer! Shouldn't they be the ones providing security?*

I tried to imagine what it would be like to run after a three-year-old boy full of energy and mischief while being eight months pregnant in a refugee camp. I remembered anticipating the birth of my second child, my only daughter. I was ecstatic to be having a girl. I was also quite nervous, not knowing if I would ever be able to love a second child as much as I had already loved my first. I knew I would deliver my daughter by a planned Cesarean section and wondered how I could care for both of them while my surgical wound was healing.

No one can adequately prepare a woman for what having a first baby feels like. Not just the actual birthing process but the aftermath of healing, the emotions, and what breastfeeding feels like or encompasses. No one adequately prepares for the experience of using the bathroom for the first time after a seven-pound human being was expelled from one's body. One believes nursing a baby comes naturally, unaware that sometimes, the baby does not latch on well. If the mother is too stressed, the baby does not nurse well; when the baby does not nurse well, the baby gets overstimulated and that makes it difficult for the baby to latch. This then worries the mother more than she already had been. In turn, these experiences may lead to a big vicious cycle.

No one can fully understand the difficulty of being a first-time mom in a refugee camp. I struggled with how these women were taking care of their hygiene postpartum in a refugee camp. It was hard for me to understand how they were keeping up with their hydration enough to be able to nurse a baby in a refugee camp. How were they trying to bond with their babies or keep their stress levels down so they could produce enough milk to nourish an entirely dependent new life?

In 2013, Angelina Jolie won the prestigious Jean Hersholt Humanitarian Award for her charitable work with UNRA (the United Nations Refugee Agency). In her acceptance speech, she said precisely what resonated in my heart as I met woman after woman at the camp[4]:

"I have never understood why some people are lucky enough to be born with the chance I had to have this path in life. And why, across the world, there's a woman just like me, with the same abilities, desires, work ethic, and love for her family, who would most likely make better films, and better speeches—only she sits in a refugee camp. She has no voice. She worries about what her children will eat, how to keep them safe, and if they'll ever be allowed to return home. I don't know why this is my life, and that's hers. I don't understand that, but I will do as my mother said and do the

best I can with this life to be of use."

At the end of a long day of seeing patients, I met a woman named Kinana, who brought in her children for upper respiratory tract infections. They were the last family I saw on this second day. I was hot, tired, sweaty, thirsty, and hungry. All I wanted to do was return to my hotel and shower.

Kinana had piercing green eyes and a fiery personality. "Just come with me. I want to show you something in my living space," she insisted. Despite my exhaustion, I knew that I had the privilege of being able to go back to my hotel soon. Kinana did not have that option. I went with her.

"I had the choice of staying in the tents or in this building that has long hallways separated by hanging plastic tarps to make rooms," she said. "I chose the building because it is closest to the bathrooms. This way, every time one of my kids gets sick with vomiting and diarrhea, at least we are close to the bathrooms."

Vomiting and diarrhea are common complaints in refugee camps. There is a lack of hygiene, and viral gastroenteritis spreads like wildfire. Although her building was closest to the bathrooms, it also had a less desirable feature. It was far less ventilated than a tent. That caused more respiratory tract infections to spread and linger. Pick your poison.

As soon as I entered her "room," the smell of mold overtook me. The heat of southern Turkey had improved in September than it had been a few months prior, but it was still over ninety degrees. Her eyes welled up with tears.

Her voice cracked. "I never imagined that one day I would leave my house and end up living like this."

She had lived an upper-middle-class life in Syria her entire life. Her husband had a stable job. She had often visited with her extended family, friends, and neighbors, so she was comfortable. And now, she was living in a warehouse, the sole adult taking care of her five children.

Her story sticks with me because she, like everyone around her, believed Syria to be stable. She was living the life that any stay-at-home mom could relate to with the daily activities of maintaining a household: cooking, cleaning up, laundry, making sure the kids do their homework, and keeping up with their studies. Suddenly, she found herself in a warehouse, unsure of what lies in store for her and her children.

Every time I remember her, it gives me pause when I think I live a stable life; I make sure my kids get to school and have clean clothes and healthy meals. I go to work every day and come home to ensure they do their homework and study for their exams. I go out with friends and relatives. I believe the country I live in is stable. Then, what differentiates me from Kinana?

CHAPTER FOUR

Realizations

Ann Arbor, USA 2011

It is shocking to witness first-hand the lives of refugees, who had suddenly been exposed to extreme poverty, violence one could never fully imagine, and unimaginable tragedies. However, I didn't realize that I would also experience another culture shock upon re-entry to my home country. People talk a lot about caring for caregivers nowadays. That was not a popular conversation in 2011. No one understood how I felt; it was quite confusing for them and me.

I returned to Ann Arbor near the end of September 2011 and immediately re-immersed in my job and caring for my two young children. A friend, Sarah, stopped for a quick visit to welcome me home.

"I am so glad you are back safe and sound." She gave me a tight squeeze. "That was really brave what you did."

"Thanks." I shrugged. "What do you have planned for the rest of the day?"

"I am going to get a haircut. What do you think if I go short this time? I think it would look cute with my small face, but my sister thinks it's too drastic!" She folded her hair onto itself to show me what it would look like. I didn't reply. That would have been a normal conversation before I went to Turkey. But after coming back, my response was to stare blankly at what she was asking me, not knowing why I suddenly felt so angry about something so small.

However, years later, I can explain it. At the time, I remembered how, one week before this moment, I spoke to a woman who was experiencing being postpartum with a newborn infant in a hot and filthy refugee camp. This woman had to ensure she got enough hydration to make breastmilk and safeguard her neonate from getting an infection while caring for her paraplegic husband. She had to ensure that her husband would not develop pressure ulcers (opening of the skin if the patient is not moved frequently throughout the day) and that those ulcers would not get infected. That would require proper nutrition, not the carbohydrate-filled meals served in refugee camps. And at that moment, my friend wanted me to comment about which hairstyle would make her face look cute. It was challenging to come to terms with having these seemingly everyday conversations after what I had just witnessed and experienced. My husband felt the same way, and I was thankful I had shared the experience with him. We understood one another, and it helped.

Secondary trauma is real. It is the phenomenon when a caregiver experiences the trauma of the person they are caring for. There are studies documenting it now. I did not know about them then, but I could have contributed to the data. When I returned from Turkey, I made it a point never to view images of massacres in Syria. I never watched the YouTube videos that were being uploaded by Syrians daily. If I ever scrolled through social media at night in bed, after the kids had gone to sleep and had a fleeting thought to click on something like that, my husband said, "Don't watch that stuff." I knew it was not good for me, but a part of me was worried about what was happening to the people of Syria.

However, one day, in March of 2012, I traveled back from Chicago to Detroit alone. While waiting to board my flight, I made the colossal mistake of clicking on an article detailing the Karm al-Zeitoun massacre that had just occurred in Syria. There was an image of two young boys lying on the floor, their faces and chests covered in blood. The older boy wore jeans and a long-sleeved multi-colored, striped shirt. He looked to be about ten years old. The younger boy beside him wore black pants, a pink jacket, and a blue shirt. He looked to be about six years old. The part of the image I do not forget was the evidence of urinary incontinence on their pants. Yes, that happens after death. However, in children, loss of bladder control also occurs in situations of extreme fear. I wondered how long they knew what would happen to them before they were massacred. It made me nauseated and overwhelmed with grief.

The next day, I went to work. I started a service week as the supervising and teaching physician for the residents at the hospital. We were checking on our long list of patients. My senior resident was a tall young man from Nigeria, a strong resident who knew what he was doing; he would graduate soon and be alone. I knew I would not have to do much to alter his management.

One of our patients was a baby with a yet-to-be-diagnosed underlying medical problem. He had a skin disorder and a suspected immunodeficiency, and he was not gaining weight properly. He had an uncomplicated surgical procedure the day before I started. The surgeon said we could let the baby feed, so we did. We examined him, and everything seemed to be progressing as expected.

Our next set of patients was on another floor, and as we continued, we heard the overhead pager. "Code Blue room 3201." Code Blue means impending cardiopulmonary arrest and that immediate medical attention is required. "Wait, isn't that our patient's room?" I said to my senior resident. "Yes, that's the baby who is post-op day 1," he replied. My team, consisting of the senior resident, two interns, a few medical students, and myself, ran up the stairs and back to his room. I was not expecting to see what I saw next.

The baby was crying. He was pale and slightly blue. His surgical wound had dehisced (come apart), his belly was wide open, and his intestines splayed out for the world to see. I froze. Not because I did not know what to do medically but because I just kept seeing the images of the massacred boys in my head. I kept repeating, "Oh my God, oh my God," in my head.

"We should call surgery," my senior resident said.

"Yes." I snapped back to reality. "Get some gauze, soak it in saline, cover his intestines, start Zosyn [an antibiotic], get a nasal cannula, and page surgery STAT!" I have never frozen in a medical emergency before. But I realized that secondary trauma is in fact a real phenomenon and, if unacknowledged or unaddressed, can be quite damaging to one's self and to the people around that person.

I never made the mistake of clicking on these images again. I needed to recognize the process of re-entry, which is necessary for one to readjust to the original circumstances to which one was accustomed. Did recognizing it help cease my internal struggles?

In Hatay, I had been working in a refugee camp surrounded by thousands of refugees, and I never realized that I, myself, was also a refugee. Having immigrated to the United States at the age of four, I had very few memories of life before our move. I grew up spending my summers playing kick the can and baseball in the street with my sister, our neighbors Debra and Kirk, and whoever else was around from the neighborhood. We did not go inside until it grew dark. If it was a rainy day, I stayed inside, either reading a book or playing Atari, which was then replaced by a Nintendo gaming console.

My favorite holiday is Thanksgiving. I always insist on hosting it for the family and a Friendsgiving early in November because the experiences in my life have made me incredibly thankful. I love celebrating Valentine's Day. A part of my rational brain tells me it is a commercialized holiday meant to make us more consumers than we already were. However, I choose to shut that part of my brain off. I have spent so much of my life as a serious student that I have decided on this day to enjoy eating chocolate hearts or pink-frosted cupcakes with my family members, letting them know how much I love them.

Every Christmas break until I moved away to college, my sister and I watched the 1954 version of *White Christmas*. I love the beautiful lights and festivities of the Christmas season. It is not like my family came to the United States and suddenly became "enlightened, integrated Americans." Syrians have a long history of sharing cross-cultural and cross-religious holidays. My parents grew up in a pluralistic Syria.

When I first went to Syria as a young teenager, one of the most famous historic sites my family visited was Sednaya, a city in the mountains seventeen miles north of the capital city, Damascus. Sednaya is one of the last places on earth where Aramaic, the language of Jesus Christ, is spoken. It is home to a large Greek Orthodox monastery, the Convent of Our Lady of Sednaya, believed to be built by the Byzantine emperor Justinian I. It is magnificent, made out of cool, yellow bricks with multiple staircases with black railings leading up to the entrance. The courtyards are tranquil, the panoramic views of the city underneath are breathtaking, and the cool breeze flowing through is welcomed in the hot Syrian summers. Muslims and Christians travel to this convent, believing the space to be holy and seeking its sanctuary for healing. In Syria, it is not uncommon for Syrian Muslims to send holiday greetings to their Syrian Christian neighbors for Christmas or Syrian Christians to greet their Muslim neighbors on the days of Islamic religious holidays.

In hindsight, I am flabbergasted that it takes a 70-year-old reality TV star running for president, capitalizing on xenophobia, racism, and Islamophobia, bolstering his ratings to remind me that I came here as a refugee. In September 2017, almost a year into Donald Trump's presidency, US Attorney General Jeff Sessions announced the end of the DACA (Deferred Action for Childhood Arrivals) program, which hurled 800,000 dreamers into a state of anxiety as they scrambled to figure out their fate. Most dreamers did not know any other country besides the United States. As the news of the unknown fate of the dreamers was described on major news outlets, I read about a group of four Harvard medical students who wrote a letter to a Boston radio station addressing their fellow Americans to speak out against the termination of DACA. In this letter, these four students made a case for why they should be allowed to stay in the United States. The students cited the doctor shortage crisis that the US is on the trajectory of encountering by 2025. The dreamers tried to prove to fellow Americans why they were worthy of having their rights protected and how fellow Americans would suffer if the 100 DACA-recipient medical students in the US lost their ability to pursue a residency and become full-fledged doctors.

Why do they have to prove their worth? Shouldn't the fact that they were human beings brought to the US by their parents (without their say or will) and that they know no other home be enough for us to embrace them and protect them? All this talk about dreamers, particularly the medical student dreamers, awakened in me a recounting of my personal history about how I came to the United States. Day and night, I kept thinking I could have been a dreamer. Thankfully, the program's termination had not gone unchecked. Several lawsuits were filed against the Trump administration for ending the program. The legal future of the DACA program remains uncertain.

CHAPTER FIVE

Trust

Hatay, Turkey 2011

During my second day of seeing patients in Hatay, Turkey, I met a fourteen-year-old girl, Rana, who forgot her glasses in Syria in all the madness of mass evacuation. Rana had been in the camps for two months, and her mom said that she had an unrelenting headache, a tearing of her eyes, and she refused to get up and leave the tent.

"Every day, I tell her to get up and walk around. Get a breath of fresh air. Maybe, you will feel better. But she refuses and says, 'my head hurts too much,'" her mom explained. As her mom and I talked, I noticed Rana kept squinting.

"Have you had her eyes checked recently?" I asked.

"No, she has glasses, but she forgot to pack them when we left."

When I was Rana's age, I wore glasses. Now, I wear contact lenses. I could not get by ten minutes of my day without my contact lenses. I talked to one of the camp's directors to ensure that Rana could see an eye doctor in Antakya, a forty-minute drive away from the camps, as soon as possible so she could replace her glasses. Simple day-to-day things we take for granted can make or break the life of a refugee.

Later, Yusuf came to see me with his five-year-old daughter, Razan. She had a history of a brain bleed and seizures. He came to me to adjust his daughter's seizure medications because she had frequent seizures. As a non-neurologist, I did the best that I could. Yusuf told me someone said that the developmental delay that Razan suffered from, would improve. After hearing his story about how he had to evacuate his family from Syria, I did not have the heart to tell him that his daughter's condition would likely not improve after suffering a brain hemorrhage.

These are the things one learns to do on medical missions. One knows how to do the best one can with what one has. One learns to relay only the necessary information. One learns to think about whether the information one is about to relay will help or cause unnecessary harm. One wonders about the impact of false hope. Is it better to believe in false hope rather than push oneself into accepting hopelessness in case of defeat? These are the questions I found myself contemplating when I had a free minute on our drives to and from the camps.

One of the most important aspects of the doctor-patient (and patient's family) relationship is trust. If the patient or family don't trust you, you can't adequately break bad news to them. Or they won't believe you if you have bad news to give them.

I tried to delve deep into what it would mean to break bad news to someone in a refugee camp. I had only experienced breaking bad news to families in the United States, where I knew where to refer the patient to next. When I went to medical school, I was briefly taught how to break the bad news to patients and how to take care of my mental health. We had one class that lasted a whole semester on talking to patients and, perhaps, a session or two on breaking the bad news.

It is essential to take the patient into a quiet room. The doctor should sit down and not be in a rush; make sure there is someone else with the patient to support them emotionally. However, all those "important" things we are taught sometimes fly out the window when it comes to actual implementation.

In 2003, for example, when I was a first-year resident working an ER shift, a set of parents brought in their three-year-old girl because she kept bumping into the walls. They thought maybe she was having trouble seeing. After discussing with my supervising doctor, I ordered a head CT. I went to look at it before the official radiology report was back. I am no radiologist, but I could see the large tumor impinging on her optic chiasm from a mile away. "Okay, go tell them," my attending said. "What?! I tell them?"

Of course, he would not let a first-year, inexperienced trainee tell these parents the most devastating news they had ever heard, right? He did not. I accompanied him as he broke the news as gently as he could. These are the encounters where we learn the art of medicine. If one is lucky, her teacher teaches her exactly how it is done.

At the end of my second full day of seeing patients in Hatay, our driver Ayman came to pick us up and take us back to the city. We found him talking to another Syrian refugee, Waleed. Ayman was Turkish, but his grandparents were from Aleppo, Syria. He had retained the ability to speak Arabic. Waleed was a Syrian journalist in his late 50s. He had an adolescent boy with cerebral palsy that caused a significant developmental delay. The Turkish government had offered to pay for the boy to enroll in a special education school three days a week in Antakya, but they would not pay for transportation. So Waleed was trying to get a job to pay for transportation.

Ayman shook his head as we drove away. "How is Waleed going to get a job as a journalist here if he does not speak Turkish?"

I tried to imagine myself in Waleed's place, trying to start over in a country where I don't speak the language, in my mid-50s. During the trip, I was still relatively young, in my mid-30s. I thought to myself, and there was no way I could do it. But then, I thought of my two children and knew I would have to manage something for their sake. I welcomed the reprieve the drive back to the hotel provided and mentally prepared for the next busy day.

Even when a pediatrician gains the trust of the patient's parents, based on my practice in the States, I already knew that children would still often mistrust doctors. Nevertheless, the fear that some Syrian refugee children exhibited in the camps was on a whole other level. I was sad about how mistrustful they were. However, given what they had been through in the past few months before arriving in Turkey, I completely understood. I saw many children in Turkey with somatic complaints, just like Dr. Zakaria had warned me about. I saw many children with abdominal pain or chest pain of no organic origin. Psychosomatic complaints in children are a recurring theme on medical missions such as the one I was on.

The camps were very close to the Syrian border. In fact, on our way from Antakya to the camps, we saw the border and Syrian land. It was hard to believe that just a half-hour away, there was a whole different world of protests, barbaric killing, bombings, shelling, sniper fire, and torture.

It was not only the children who were mistrustful. The adults were as well. If their government tried to kill them, I imagined it would be difficult not to be mistrustful. I am not going to lie; it had even been hard to trust everyone I met in Hatay (especially close to the border). Knowing what I knew about Syrian politics, it was hard not to doubt people's intentions. However, I was trying my hardest to focus on the humanitarian mission I came for and to give people the benefit of the doubt.

My husband and I split from the other three doctors on our last day there. We had Ayman take us back to the first refugee camp we had visited. I had a couple of patients to whom I promised to bring back some medication, and I wanted to say goodbye to one of the women I befriended. It was taking longer than usual to arrive at our destination. My husband fell asleep in the back of the car, and I sat silently next to him, looking around, trying to figure out if we were going in the right direction. Again, I saw the border crossing into Syria and was too worried to sit silently. I nudged my husband, Amjad.

"Huh? What happened?" He mumbled.

"It's taking way longer to get there than the past few days," I whispered.

Ayman did not speak English, and I did not want him to understand my worries.

"What do you mean?"

"I mean, I am not sure where we are, and I don't know why it is taking so long to get there."

I started to have images of being taken across the border and imprisoned for helping political enemies of the state. It was no secret that the Syrian government had punished physicians and other healthcare workers who had aided wounded protesters. *What if I never see my kids again? Or my parents? Or my sister?*

"So, just ask him," Amjad said.

Finally, I asked Ayman, in Arabic, why it was taking so long.

"I took an alternate route because it's lunchtime, high traffic time here in Hatay. We'll be there in fifteen minutes," Ayman replied.

I translated for my husband. Amjad's family originates from the Indian subcontinent. He is fluent in Urdu and knows a few words of Arabic that relate to rearing small children but not enough to understand the conversation I was having with Ayman.

"See. Nothing to worry about." He dozed right back off to sleep. I love how he can do that. He zonks out in the middle of me thinking we were off to our deaths or through the wailing of our colicky baby.

Just as promised, we arrived outside the barbed wire surrounding the camps fifteen minutes later. We showed our passports and government-issued ID cards and were allowed in by the Turkish military officers. The refugees were not allowed to roam freely outside of the camps. These are the details that no one highlighted when we watched the news in the States.

The conditions in the camps were unpleasant. These people left their homes to be treated like prisoners in a dusty, dirty, hot city of tents where food and life are the same day after day. In the age of smartphones, where everything could be captured on video or photo and be sent back to their friends and families back home, the conditions were open and obvious. Nevertheless, hundreds of thousands of people chose to make the journey. One only does that if the circumstances at home are dangerous.

When we returned to Chicago, my two-year-old son kept repeating, "I want to go back to Hamza's house in Michigan." Even though, by then, both his dad and I were with him. Even though he had spent the last ten days spoiled by his paternal grandparents, he just wanted to return to his home. My heart was warmed by how he referred to himself in the third person. Looking at his little face, I could not help but think of all the children I saw in the camps. They must have also said they wanted to return to their homes in Syria. I wondered how the refugee parents answered their children who posed such difficult questions. Did they, themselves, know the answers?

CHAPTER SIX

Refuge?

When I read Zaher's message about crossing the Red Sea to Yemen, all I could see in my mind's eye were images I had conjured up listening to the stories of Syrian refugees I treated in Greece in the summer of 2016.

"You have to understand, no one puts their children in a boat unless the water is safer than the land," wrote the British-Somali poet, Warsan Shire: "No one leaves home unless home is the mouth of a shark. You only run for the border when you see the whole city running as well." Or, in Syria's case... multiple cities.

Chicago, USA 2016

Just a few short months before my arrival in Greece, the small body of three-year-old Aylan Kurdi washed up on a Turkish shore. He was wearing blue shorts and a red t-shirt. When I saw his image on the nightly news, it burned my heart. It was not lost upon me that just the day before, I had posted a picture of my then two-year-old son wearing the same blue shorts and t-shirt, and he was running after a squirrel—*the irony*. I could not erase the image of Aylan's corpse from my head. All I could do to soothe the pain was to get on a plane, alone and go to a place I had never been to before, where I did not speak the language of the land, with complete trust that if I intended to help people, the path would be cleared for me. And in fact, it was clear enough.

Ten days before I was to travel to Greece, I decided to crowdsource for donations. I expected to collect $1,000 at best. I was shocked by the generosity of my friends and that of their friends because I spent fifteen minutes putting the website together, posting a few pictures from my trip to Turkey five years earlier. I was now a mother of three young children under seven. I was working as a joint pediatric infectious disease and pediatric hospitalist physician. Spare time was not a luxury afforded to people like me. In those ten days, I managed to collect $15,000 for the refugees in Greece. I paid my way for the journey there. It was the least I could do.

By the summer of 2016, images the media called "migrants" walking in groups of hundreds across Europe were all over the news. More than one million human beings crossed into Europe in 2015, sparking what the media called a "refugee crisis" and creating deep divides in the European Union. The largest source of these people was Syria. But people also fled ongoing violence in Afghanistan, Iraq, and other countries.

The word "migrant" irritated me. It gave the illusion that someone was moving for better opportunities or making more money. It did not paint an accurate picture of people fleeing barrel bombs raining down upon them, chemical weapons suffocating them, and human rights violations like sodomy and electrocution torturing them. I knew that was what the Syrian people were fleeing from. Syrians were not leaving because they wanted to make an extra dollar.

Thessaloniki, Greece 2016

My first day on the pediatric side in Thessaloniki, Greece, was a little slow. That allowed me to talk to some of the refugees that my friend Laura, an internal medicine physician from London, was seeing. While she prepared their medications or wrote in their medical record, I asked them how they arrived in Greece, who came with them, or just in general, what their story was. Many talked about the places they had sought refuge in before they finally ended up in Greece. Stories of being smuggled from town to town across Syria before finally arriving in Turkey and taking a raft across the sea to Greece. They talked about all the money they gave to the different smugglers. Many had family members who left before them; usually, the men who had made it to Germany to scope out the scene and then, once established with a decent lifestyle, called for their families to join them. As for the families who followed, the borders began to close with no way out.

I met an elderly grandmother who brought in her seven-month-old grandchild for a ruptured tympanic membrane (nasty ear infection where the ear drum breaks). She told me her son (the baby's father) was in Germany, and they called him daily.

"My son cries because he misses his children. His kids cry because they miss their father, and I cry because I am heartbroken at the condition of my son and his kids," she said in a quivering tone of voice.

Then, I met an eleven-year-old girl, Suzan, who had a history of congenital heart disease that was repaired in infancy in Syria. Her dad brought her on my first day because he thought that somehow, me being a new face, I could help him get her seen faster by the cardiologist. Most of the volunteer healthcare workers who had been coming to the refugee camps in Thessaloniki were general practitioners. Patients who needed a specialist were referred through the Greek system. Since the Greek medical system was so overwhelmed with its population, there was a seemingly endless waiting period for the Syrian refugees to see a specialist.

Suzan's dad described the symptoms of his daughter's weak heart: shortness of breath and difficulty walking for long periods. I felt helpless because I knew there was nothing I could do to make her appointment come sooner. The dad, himself, was waiting to be seen by a cardiologist. He was recently diagnosed with cluster headaches and was prescribed a drug called verapamil. The volunteer physicians could get the medicine for him. However, in that case, the father had to obtain a screening or EKG to ensure his heart was healthy before taking the drug. A month before I arrived, a cardiologist was doing EKGs at one of the other camps. He planned to get screened but was asked to take two pediatric patients with him (kids unrelated to him). He took them and went to the other camp.

"I let the kids go first because they are children, and by the time it was my turn to get the EKG, the EKG machine had run out of paper. I lost my chance, and who knows when the next cardiologist will come." I felt sad about his hopelessness and angry at my inability to help him since I was not a cardiologist and did not have an EKG machine. I could not move his place in line to see a Greek cardiologist.

I hung out for a little bit with his daughter, Suzan, the next day. This was the same girl with a history of congenital heart disease, shortness of breath, and exercise intolerance. She described how difficult it was to breathe through the tear gas sprayed at her multiple times throughout her family's journey. Eleven years old, with heart disease, experiencing war, bombs, tear gas, and became a refugee. At the age of eleven, shouldn't the world have been wide open for her?

I met another man, Ali, who was either my age or a little older. The adults looked older due to hardship, while the children looked younger due to malnutrition. Ali was waiting to see my colleague for infected insect bites. I could see his legs riddled with red bumps between where his navy green capris ended and his ankle socks began. Many refugees, adults, and children have suffered due to the mosquito population. On top of not having a bed to sleep on, a pillow to rest their heads on, or the oppressive heat they tried to sleep through, the mosquitoes ate them alive. As he was waiting for his medical record to be updated, I chit-chatted with him.

"Who are you here with?"

"My wife. She is my second wife." He hesitated, deciding if he was going to tell me the rest. "My first wife...well, a barrel bomb fell on our house, and the only thing that remained of her were morsels of flesh splattered all over the place," he said quickly, with a sort of nervous smile on his face as if to say, *I better say this fast and get out of here before I have to process it.* He said it as if it were so typical. However, as soon as he said it, I could tell that he was done conversing with me.

What does one reply to that? How does one react to that? If I had been trained in mental health, I might have delved deeper, and his emotions would have come flooding out. But I am not, so I did not. *No one should ever see another human being's flesh splattered all over the place, and indeed not the closest human being to him,* I thought.

Over the next few days, pediatric attendance at the camp clinics had increased quite a bit from day one. I saw patients with URIs (upper respiratory tract infections), asthma exacerbations, vomiting and diarrhea, fever, and conjunctivitis.

Many stories still stick out in my head. The worst is the haunted eyes of the refugees. Just as their memories went on repeat, so do their stories in my mind, even to this day.

I saw a 45-day-old infant with bronchiolitis. He had been my youngest patient thus far, although I knew younger patients were in the camps. I knew because I had to send a woman by ambulance to the hospital when she reported that her water broke and she was 39 weeks pregnant. A newborn baby. In a refugee camp. Dirt and dust everywhere. An epidemic of chain smokers in a massive warehouse with little ventilation. I did not think it was healthy to be there, let alone an immunocompromised newborn baby.

There were many infants at the camp. A young couple brought in their three-month-old because she had thrush (fungal infection) on her tongue. Thrush can be seen in normal infants and persists if the pacifier and bottle nipples are not sterilized appropriately (nearly impossible prospects in a refugee camp). I started her on the treatment, but the parents brought her back within 48 hours because she was not latching on and nursing well from the mother. At first, only the dad came in with the baby.

"Have you tried to feed her from a bottle?" I asked him.

"Yes," he said. "She takes it just fine. She will drink two to three ounces from the bottle, but when my wife puts her to breastfeed, she cries."

I could not help but think back to my days as a first-time mom trying to nurse my newborn baby boy and how nerve-wracking it was.

I asked him. "Does the mom get anxious or frustrated when trying to nurse the baby?"

He looked at me like I was the biggest idiot ever to walk the planet. "Doctor, don't you think anyone living under these conditions for months on end with no end in sight would be anxious and frustrated?!"

I had no answer for that. I felt stupid for even asking.

It was not all sadness and frustration, however. There were many moments when I was utterly in awe of how some could make a waterfall out of the rain. Yousuf, a middle-aged man from the city of Homs, collected any metal fragments he found around the camps. He melted the metal and made it into jewelry to sell. Entrepreneurship was alive and well in the camps. Kareem opened a coffee stand. I frequented his stand and bought anything he was making, more to support him than for anything else. Khaled used to own two very lucrative restaurants in Syria before fleeing the war. He started a fantastic falafel stand in the camps—crunchy balls of ground chickpeas mixed with a kick of cumin. The falafel was soft on the inside, a result of being deep-fried, drizzled with creamy tahini sauce, tucked into a warm pita, and topped with fresh Persian cucumbers and succulent tomatoes. It was one of the best sandwiches I had ever tasted.

It was not all business, either. I saw a former electrician who had jerry-rigged an old car motor he found and converted it into a fan for his pregnant wife! If that isn't love, I don't know what is!

On the other hand, there were many cases of psychological complaints. A woman came to talk to me about her twelve-year-old daughter, who suffered from nocturnal enuresis (wetting the bed at night, common in kids under stress). I told her why she probably had it.

"What's the solution to this problem?" The mother asked me.

"There are some NGOs (non-governmental organizations) in the area doing psychosocial work with the children, but I don't know how often they are available. I will check for you."

I also did not know how many sessions each child was allowed and how effective this type of therapy was without continuity. All I could tell this worried mother was that, hopefully, with much reassurance and safety, the nocturnal enuresis would improve. Did I believe this? Yes. However, could I imagine this family relocating to a safe place with regular daily routines re-established anytime soon? No. I said a little silent prayer for her family.

Nocturnal enuresis was not the only ramification of stress. The women told me how so many children cried at night, especially when they heard a loud noise because they remembered the bombs. In such a world, we have failed them.

Sometimes, I would post some of these reflections in real-time on social media. People asked me why I was not posting pictures. Others were encouraging me to put up pictures with my posts. In the era of social media and short attention spans, one seems compelled to post images that grab the reader's/viewer's attention. Honestly, I had been too embarrassed to ask any of the refugees I encountered if I could take their picture. I felt that taking a photo of them in their current horrible conditions and posting them would continue to rob them of their dignity. On so many levels and at so many places along their journeys, they had been humiliated. I translated one woman's journey for a friend, Anna, a communications student working on an audio piece about the refugee experience for her local radio station. I could not count the number of times the interview subject used the word *itbahdalna*.

Arabic is a very nuanced language, so *itbahdalna*, in this context, means a combination of "we were exhausted and humiliated." She said it as she described when things started to go badly for her family in Homs and how they hid in different homes, jumping over walls to get where they needed to go. They found places to sleep on their way to Damascus, returned to Homs, and traveled to Qamishli. *Itbahdalna*. Finally, they decided to leave for Turkey, having to borrow money. *Itbahdalna*. Having to cross the barbed wire border, pants tearing while being shot. *Itbahdalna*. They were stranded at a hotel for days on end by the smuggler before being allowed on a raft. *Itbahdalna*.

Some of the refugees wanted their pictures taken and their stories heard because they believed that there was no other way someone would be able to learn about the horrors they had encountered, see the conditions they had lived in, and continue to keep the borders closed. If I believed that taking a picture would let just one refugee family out of the camps, I would have taken and posted thousands of them.

On my fifth day in Thessaloniki, I went to a different camp than the one I had been going to for the first four days. Not much was different in the new camp. Long rows of tents. Dirt. Dust. Disease. Despair. One thing that haunted me the most about the refugee children was that I saw my kids and sometimes, my childhood in them. Like when a dad brought in his two young daughters, aged four and two. The four-year-old was holding her sister's hand and trying to make her little sister laugh, and the little sister giggled non-stop. It was such a beautiful encounter to watch, and she reminded me of my older sister and how protective she was of me. The little girl's giggles were music to my ears because I had not heard a child's laughter for almost four days straight, even though hundreds of children were around.

The stories of separation were unbearable. One dad, Zeyad, brought in his eleven-year-old son to see me. I asked him how many kids he had.

"I have four, but only three are with me at the camp."

Did I really want to know? Sniper? Bomb? Arrested? Lost? Kidnapped? He told me anyway.

"When we left Syria, my sister, her husband, and their kids also left with our family. After we finally made it to Greece, my wife and I wanted to rest, but my sister's family wanted to go on. My nine-year-old daughter, Aneesa, begged me to go with her aunt and cousins. I let her go because I knew we would catch up to them. Except we didn't. We couldn't. The borders closed that night."

"How awful!"

"We Skype with her every day. She is in school in Germany. She just celebrated her 10th birthday." He showed me a picture of her blowing out the candles. Without her mother. Without her father. Without her siblings.

"I am happy for her. She is in a stable place, and most importantly, she is going to school." The tears were welling up in his eyes and mine.

This encounter moved me to Skype my own family. I heard my two-year-old son, Zaid, in the background. He had just woken up from his nap and was a little cranky. He listened to my husband talking, and he recognized my voice. When he came on Skype, he kept whimpering. "Mama, coming? Mama, coming?" I could say, "Yes, in four days, Mama is coming." How many refugee children wonder if their mom or dad are ever coming back? Do children know whether their parents had been separated due to displacement, arrest, or murder? How many can give an exact number of days before their union?

Moving forward, I was banned from talking to my Zaid until my return.

"If you want to listen to him running and talking, you can do that all you want, but you can't talk to him anymore. It's getting too hard to console him every time you hang up, Sweetheart. It's not fair on him or me." My husband told me.

My husband, Amjad, was such a trooper. It was not easy holding down the fort when the two-year-old did not understand and kept asking where his mama was and when she was coming back.

During a slow period, some of our volunteers went out to run some errands, and I sat at our triage desk. You hear that we have a triage area and cannot help your mind imagining an ER triage in a nice big, clean, well-lit, air-conditioned hospital. But no. It was just a table and chairs, paper and pen, thermometer, and pulse ox. Still hot. Still dusty.

I registered a woman, Samya, who was there to see the internal medicine doctor. As she waited for her turn, I asked her about her journey. Samya and her husband had three kids, aged six, four, and two, similar to my seven, five, and two-year-old at that time. Most refugees had been in the camps for six months since I visited Greece, and Samya's journey started in the winter. She described getting across the Syrian border as a similar story to others. However, when they ran out of money and could no longer afford to be smuggled, they had to walk for two days in the cold and snow.

"The region we had to cross was mountainous. I carried the two-year-old, and my husband carried the four-year-old. But what could we do? The six-year-old had to walk on his own." Six years old. Walking for two days straight. In snow. I did not think my seven-year-old could have done it. I did not know I could have even handled watching him go through with it.

All the refugees in the camps in Greece talked about the smugglers. Human beings who smuggle other human beings. Let that sink in for a minute. In some ways, I am so glad they exist. Their existence has been one of the few, if not the only, ways the Syrian people have been able to flee the atrocities in Syria, trying to seek refuge. But how is drowning at sea, border closures or being locked up in a refugee camp real refuge?

CHAPTER SEVEN

The Snipers

On my last day at the camp clinic in Thessaloniki, I was overwhelmed with sadness. Sadness at the situation my fellow human beings had to endure. Sadness about my time helping them being over. Sadness at their hopelessness as there was no end to the border closures. I tried to be uplifting, especially when I saw a sixteen-year-old girl named Samah, complaining of a headache. She was as sharp as a nail.

After I introduced myself, I asked, "What's up?" because that is what I usually say in the States when I see a teenager.

Without missing a beat, she replied, "I live in a refugee camp with every day being the same as the one before; what do you think is going to be up?"

Maybe when I was younger, I might have been offended by that comment. I mean, I was only there to help. Why give me the attitude? It isn't my fault that the refugee camps exist!

However, I felt like she had been right. Every day meant boredom, and on top of that, dirt, dust, heat, diseases, disgusting port-a-potties that they used as bathrooms and showers, and the same food every week. Some refugees told me: "So-and-so who came with us went back to Syria with his family."

What? I imagined going through the journey in reverse, back to an area where it is raining barrel bombs. I could not even understand that. And many said, "Well, at least the bomb falls on you, and you die with your dignity instead of this humiliation."

On that final day in Thessaloniki, my friend, Anna, asked me if I had time to translate for her radio piece describing the plight of the Syrian refugees in Europe. Easy enough, I thought, since I am fluent in Arabic. I did not anticipate the emotional toll it would take on me from listening to and then relaying real-life horror stories. She had chosen two women to do a live interview with and would do an audio recording of their voices.

Both were Syrian Kurds. The first woman, Rama, had nine children, one of whom was a young man who was killed. She had one child who was imprisoned and one child who had fled to Germany. The one in Germany had four bullets lodged in him, and a five-year-old boy Rama was taking care of in the refugee camps. Her daughter was married off at a young age, but because of the conflict, she was divorced. Anna did not press her about what that meant. Did the son-in-law join the Free Syrian Army? Was the stress of the conflict spilling over into their marital life? It was not clear.

Rama said one of the most depressing things, "I don't know anything about my arrested son. That is worse than anything else I have been through. It is worse than finding out my other son was killed and worse than being in these camps."

Many Syrians had little to no information on their arrested loved one(s). I guessed it was one thing if the missing family member was dead, and one knows that, like some sense of closure. But I gathered, based on Rama's interview, that it was a different thing to keep wondering: *Is he being tortured every day? If he is alive, chances are that is true. Will he ever be released? Will I ever get to hug my son again? Ever? Will I ever kiss him? Smell him? Or is he already dead? Did they bury him or throw his body away like they did the trash?* During my time in Greece and my existence as a Syrian, I have heard many stories of Syrian security forces disposing of bodies without a proper burial, tombstone, or trace.

Rama's eyes were empty. Her eyelids were perpetually swollen. Despite the journey out of Syria and the difficulties of the living conditions at the refugee camps, I asked her multiple times throughout the interview, "Is there anything someone could provide for you that would make your daily living here better?"

"No, I want this situation to end so I can return home."

"Really? There is nothing somebody could buy for you here to help you?" I reiterated.

"No, I just want this situation to be over so I can return to my Syrian neighborhood."

"How about a mosquito zapper?" I suggested.

She laughed. "Where would I plug it in?"

Good point. I would have had a long list of things I could identify that would make my living situation in a refugee camp more tolerable—*such resilience in the face of such unbelievable adversity.*

Surprisingly, she had one request: "Will you broadcast my voice over Turkish airwaves? Maybe my [missing] son managed to escape, and if he hears my voice, he will come to Greece." The hope and desperation in her voice were unmistakable.

The second woman we talked to, Khadija, wanted to protect her anonymity. She disagreed on being recorded, and her real name used, for example. Anna could only take notes for her interview. She spoke for quite a long time about everything she saw. One portion of her story stood out:

"The situation was terrible in Homs [their city of origin]. Every day, we heard the bombs falling and the bullets flying. My husband left for work, and the kids and I sometimes hid in the bathroom to avoid sniper bullets. Even though the refrigerator was a few feet away, some days, we were too scared to come out of the bathroom to get something to eat. Despite the hunger, it was just too dangerous."

Khadija had a bubbly personality. She smiled a lot. She could be the friend anyone turns to when they need to smile after a hard day.

She said they tried to keep the kids going to school as long as possible. However, eventually, checkpoints were opened along the kids' routes to school. The military searched the kids' backpacks, asking them if they were hiding bombs there.

"The bodies of the dead killed by sniper fire could not be retrieved because people were scared they would be killed if they went out into the street. When the kids started seeing dead people in the streets, they started getting scared and having nightmares. And so, finally, I stopped sending them to school."

When she talked about the sniper fire, I flashed back to a cold winter morning in my kitchen in Ann Arbor four years prior.

Ann Arbor, USA 2011

It was 7:30 in the morning. I felt the cold kitchen tiles underneath my feet, and a draft came through the window. It was a good day for oatmeal, so I made some for my family. My cell phone rang, and I saw my dad's number on the caller ID. *Uh oh. Something must be wrong because he never calls me this early.*

"Hello?"

"Good morning, Nour," his tone was severe.

"Good morning, Baba. How are you?"

"I have been better."

"What's going on?" I was worried.

"Your cousin, Lama, was shot and killed by a sniper while she was crossing the street in Homs today."

"What?!"

"Yes, your aunt just called me this morning."

Sweet Lama. I was in utter disbelief.

I remembered the last time I saw Lama, one year ago. That was the last time I visited Syria, in January of 2010. I wish I had known back then that it would be my last visit and the last time I saw Lama. I would have soaked it in more instead of counting the days until I left. That was never my experience in Syria before, but this trip was different. It was the first time I had visited Syria as a mother and the first time I had been there in the winter. I accompanied my mom to her mother's funeral and brought along my 14-month-old son, Hamza.

Syria does not have freezing winters, but it seemed harsh for a spoiled American girl who did not remember experiencing anything besides central heat and hot water 24/7. I also had never cared that the sidewalks in Homs were so uneven and lopsided. I found that a part of its old city charm. I had never noticed that there was hardly a ramp to be seen until I had to maneuver a stroller all over the place.

My last memory of Lama was of her taking me on a shopping trip during that visit to get a pair of comfortable shoes because I had mistakenly packed a pair of shoes that I thought would be comfortable enough. However, it turned out that they were not. We had taken a taxi, and she played the Syrian version of Pat-A-Cake with my son as the driver weaved in and out of traffic. I remember her laughing with her sisters at my lack of bargaining skills. If one does not bargain in Syrian shops, a) everyone knows one is a foreigner b) one gets swindled. My cousins already knew that about me, so when I finally decided on a pair of ballet flats, Lulu (as we affectionately referred to Lama) said, "Don't talk. I will get a good deal for you."

Alas, those shoes did not turn out to be as comfortable as they were in those three seconds I had them on in the store. Either way, I kept them because they were my last memory of Lulu, and whenever I saw them, I thought about her and her smile.

Lama was a little older than I, and a mother of three school-aged children. She had never participated in a protest in her life. She was crossing the street to join her family when they got into a car, and a sniper aimed, fired, and shot her. Her husband and children got her into the car and tried to rush her to a hospital. She bled to death onto her kids' laps and died en route. When I picture Lama in my head, I always see her round face, pale complexion, and big brown eyes. She has a grin from ear to ear. I had never seen her without that grin, despite whatever she was going through. Now, I imagine her in Heaven with that same ear-to-ear grin.

Thessaloniki, Greece 2016

In Greece, Khadija continued, "I kept telling my husband, 'Let's get out of here [Homs].' But he kept insisting, 'I still have a steady job, and we are not involved in the conflict. We are not on either side (non-military and not from the Arab Sunnis who were being targeted by the military).'" She proceeded. "I fought with him every day about leaving, but he was stubborn, so we didn't leave.

"One day, I was on the rooftop of one of my friends' buildings which overlooked where my husband worked. The paramilitary forces came in and arrested twelve men. They handcuffed them and put them in the trunks of large Cadillacs." She continued. "Everybody knew the men taken away were assumed to be slaughtered like lambs.

"My friend's five-year-old daughter was with us. She saw the soldiers arresting a bearded man who always gave the kids candy. He was so kind to the children in the neighborhood. He was tall and stocky, so they had difficulty fitting him in, but they just continued stuffing him in. That was the turning point for me."

I lost it during that part of the translation. I had held it together that whole time, but when I was translating that part, I could not continue without bursting into tears.

After I composed myself, I turned to my friend, "Anna, I know this sounds unbelievable, as if this lady is making it up. Or that she is dramatizing or that maybe, it's a bad horror movie she saw and is relaying the scenes from the movie, but the reality is that many people from different areas of Syria have witnessed the same thing. Perhaps one day, these crimes will be tried at an International War Crimes

Tribunal, and people will collect these corroborated stories."

After Khadija had been speaking for about an hour, Anna tried to clarify something with her. "So, was this last part about ISIS?" She laughed. "We haven't even gotten to when ISIS started terrorizing the population."

> no one chooses refugee camps
> or strip searches where your
> body is left aching
> or prison,
> because prison is safer
> than a city of fire
> and one prison guard
> in the night
> is better than a truckload
> of men who look like your father
> no one could take it
> no one could stomach it
> no one's skin would be tough enough
>   --Warsan Shire

When one sees the images on TV of thousands of people walking thousands of miles, trying to cross into one's country, one wonders why that is happening. Remember, this woman was trying to flee Homs. Remember the men being stuffed into the trunks of cars being hauled off to be slaughtered like lambs. Remember to talk to a refugee. I dare you.

CHAPTER EIGHT

Following the Flock

Have you ever had an experience where you could pinpoint the very moment when something completely horrible started? In Greece, I felt like there was one moment that I could identify when a teenager seemed as if he were about to follow the flock that would not lead to anything good for him.

Adam was a seventeen-year-old young man residing in the refugee camps of Greece. His English was excellent. He had been hired as a translator by the NGO I volunteered with, and Adam relished his job. He was good at it, so he got to hang out with the volunteer healthcare workers quite a bit. In Greece, as in Turkey, the refugees were not allowed out of the camps without permission. Because Adam was working as a translator, he had earned this privilege. He went out to lunch with us.

Our team of multiple physicians, dental students, translators, and volunteers, who were spread out among three different camps, met in the town center for lunch daily. It was a welcomed reprieve because the cafe was air-conditioned in contrast to the small clinic areas where we worked, and the bathrooms were clean.

Like the other refugees, Adam shared stories of how the war in Syria affected his life. He had to stop going to school. Many of his family members were arrested, tortured, and suffered. His home was bombed, and his dad was killed. Now, he was the head of the family and had to protect his mom and sister. His job as a translator was to help bring income to the family.

Adam described the journey crossing the sea, corroborating the stories of the others about the human smugglers who would sometimes lie and steal their money. Some smugglers drug them, so it would be easier to stuff more people on a rubber dinghy; thus, the smugglers could make more money.

"They gave us life jackets, but I don't think they worked. The smuggler made us believe he was coming because he initially rode with us on the dinghy. We felt safer knowing he was there because an expert rode with us. Most of us did not know how to swim." He stopped to take a sip of his chocolate milkshake. "But it was pitch black. We all had to leave at night because it afforded the best opportunity not to be caught by the Turkish military. Only twenty minutes into the journey at sea, a little power boat pulled up to the dinghy and picked up the smuggler. He spoke. 'Good luck!' Then, he waved goodbye. When we screamed, 'Where are you going?' He just replied, 'You will be fine. The tide will get you to Greece, where people will take you in, and you will be safe.' And that was the last time we ever saw him." With this, he took a bite of his burger.

"What options did we have except to believe him and pray that our dinghy makes it across safely and soundly?" He asked as if there was an answer. Adam described, with meticulous detail, the wailing babies and the people vomiting into the middle of the dinghy because they were seasick. He described how cold they got as the waves came crashing into the dinghy in the dark of night.

I heard the anger in his voice when he asked, "Where was the international community when that happened to us? Where was the UN? Where were the defenders of democracy? All people in Syria wanted was the right to a democratically-elected government!" His voice started rising, and everyone in the cafe looked at him. "Where were the champions of human rights? Don't *we* have the right to live in dignity?"

Like Adam, many kids I met in Greece had faced disappointment after disappointment. The world had abandoned them. No one should grow up with this much trauma, torture, and neglect. *No kid should* watch his mom be slaughtered, his sister raped, and his dad arrested. When entities promise a vulnerable kid they will be there for them and have their back, it should be no shock that a disillusioned group of kids flock around that one representative and pledge allegiance to these groups. In some ways, Adam is no different from the teenagers I used to volunteer with at the Inner-city Muslim Action Network (IMAN – the organization the FBI interrogated me about), whom we tried to keep out of the gangs by engaging and supporting them.

This was what I saw in Adam.

Perhaps, the conflict in Syria seemed like it was none of our business (by our, I mean citizens of Europe and the United States). In reality, conflicts like those in Syria that produced refugees were an issue of national and international security. As Americans, we should not continue to put our heads in the sand and victimize ourselves by saying, "Why do they hate us?" These kids who have the potential to be the prime fodder for ISIS do not hate us. They are a product of unbelievable environmental factors of violence and abandonment, which can potentially fodder followers of ISIS.

Adam ultimately made a case for himself, his mom, and his sister and made it out of Greece. He was resettled in Frankfurt, Germany. Some of the people I became friends with in Greece had also friended him on Facebook. From time to time, they shared his videos or his posts, and I was relieved to see that he was no longer the same angry teenager I had met in Thessaloniki. He was continuing his education and working in Germany. He was bright, enthusiastic, hopeful, and had made many German friends. He had learned the language well and became fluent. He participated in festivals and cross-cultural events. He made his own social media platform to keep the dialogue going about the refugees still in the camps. He did not want people to forget about them. Just because he made it out and was again able to experience the joys of life, he did not want to forget those who were left behind. He was compelled to help those who might come after him and his family, trying to escape the same dangers he had faced in seeking safety and security.

Likewise, although I felt angry at the international community, the lack of empathy, humanity, and action, the volunteers I had met in Greece gave me hope. People from different religions, ethnicities, age groups, and walks of life had left the safety, security, and comfort of their homes to attempt to alleviate a fraction of the suffering the refugees face. Waseem, an Irish-Lebanese family practitioner and father of two, sometimes shared my clinic room, which was divided by a barrier. He saw the adults while I saw the children. Of course, I always heard his conversations with the patients. He was encouraging and listened empathetically to every single patient complaint. Then, there was Maram, a Syrian-Canadian university student who spent more than a month in Thessaloniki and kept extending her trip. She was serving as a translator. Maram tried to keep things light-hearted, but I could sometimes tell the trauma she was hearing was too much. But she returned to work every day even though she did not have to. Then, there was Mohammad, a successful young Moroccan-French man working in the financial sector in Sweden and doing quite well. Also, working as a translator, the experience of being among refugees had him questioning his trajectory in life. Then there was Laura, a medical trainee from London, who was not on her first or last medical mission when she was in Greece. She never complained, no matter how long the day was or how hot it got. She always served with a smile, and her laugh was infectious.

There were so many more volunteers. They were my tribe. It did not matter that we grew up continents apart, spoke different languages, and had completely different life experiences. Something connected our souls. Moreover, I felt comforted in being around them.

Early the following day, I was about to leave Thessaloniki. I checked out of the hotel. It was a family-owned, small hotel, and the owners gave people who had come to volunteer in the refugee camps a discount. As I checked out, I thanked the owner for hosting me and for the discount, and he thanked me for coming to help. The Greek economy and medical system were strained before the refugees showed up, and now they have become even more strained. But the Greek people were so kind and displayed the utmost hospitality and generosity. The hotel owner gestured upward, conveying that God would reward me for my humanitarian work. I verbalized the same prayer for him, and even though we did not share the same faith, at that moment, we both silently acknowledged that none of that mattered. That what united us was far greater than what made us different. And I did not need to speak his language to understand him at his core.

I had spent another week, undistracted, in a refugee camp, treating hundreds of refugees and inspired by their stories. I left there just as I came, an American physician and mom of three.

I had planned to spend a few days in Turkey with some of my Michigan friends, who were on vacation there before I returned to Chicago, where I resided. I had completed my training in Ann Arbor and worked in Detroit for three years when my husband found himself between jobs; our eldest son was on the brink of entering the school system. We hit a fork in the road: would we continue living in Michigan or move back to our city of origin? We both got recruited to jobs in Chicago, so we moved to Chicago in the Fall of 2012.

I was not going to make the same mistake of instant re-entry after my mission to Greece as I had when I went on my first mission to Hatay. I flew to Turkey. Upon encountering my friends, I had one rule: we could not talk about the experience. I did not want to talk about what I discovered in Greece. My friends were accommodating. We discussed jobs, family, and children, but the subject of the mission was off-limits. That did not mean I did not intermittently cry. I did. And they gave me the space to do that without the intrusive questions.

Little things triggered memories of my refugee encounters. We went out to eat at a family-owned restaurant: "Everything they serve here is organic and straight from the family's farm." My friend boasted. "This place has the best food around here."

When the waiter took our order, another friend suggested, "Nour, you should try the lamb here. It is so good because the meat is fresh from their farm. They raise and slaughter the sheep themselves." Slaughtered sheep. The tears came flooding out as I imagined the men stuffed into the trunks of the Cadillacs. I could not seem to stop sobbing. I had to excuse myself. I found the bathroom, where I washed my face and composed myself. When I returned to the table, I was relieved that my friends pretended I did not just start randomly sobbing. We proceeded to share a meal.

I flew home and dove right back into parenting and my job. I was grateful that both required so much of me; there was not time or room for much else. But I never forgot. The memories of my time in Thessaloniki remain as clear as if I went there yesterday.

CHAPTER NINE

They Won't Remember

I don't know why it had never occurred to me before that I was a refugee. Perhaps, it was because I came to the United States when I was so young, four years old, to be exact. Maybe it was because I had no tangible memories of my life back in Syria. It could be because the political climate was not as harsh for refugees back in 1981 as it had become. But when candidate Donald Trump's rhetoric about refugees and migrants was blaring all over the television and on the radio in the summer of 2016, I realized he was talking about people like me. It was a shocking realization. It was like waking up to a new reality of who I had always been.

My father fled from Syria in 1980. He sought and was granted asylum and lived a whole year in the United States before my mom, sister, and I were awarded a visa. He was imprisoned in Homs several times before he finally decided enough was enough. He barely talked about his time in prison, but everyone knew anyone who entered a Syrian prison was tortured.

One thing my sister and I learned never to do was to take him by surprise at night because it triggered my dad. If we ever came home late, we went straight to our rooms and never knocked on my parent's bedroom door. We were super loud if we saw the kitchen light on as we drove up the driveway to park in the garage. If my dad was in the kitchen, he knew it was just us and not a Syrian secret agent coming to pick him up in the middle of the night. The worst thing was if he woke up unexpectedly late at night because of a loud sound; he jumped out of bed so high up he almost touched the ceiling. My mom eventually told us it was because the young men in Syria were usually arrested in the middle of the night.

The only encounter my father ever shared with me about his time in Syria's prison was when he recognized one of his torturers. He was a father to one of Dad's patients. My dad was also a pediatrician. After his residency in the United States, he returned to Syria and had a thriving practice. The line would be so long to see him that it wound around the block. When my dad recognized his torturer in disbelief, the man said, "I am sorry, Doctor, it's just my job."

Even though many years had passed, the hurt and betrayal of being tortured by someone whose baby he had taken care of were evident in how his forehead wrinkled. The corners of his eyebrows turned down as he relayed the incident.

The only memory I have of when we first moved to the United States is of how emotional my dad was when we finally arrived at the airport in Chicago. How much he hugged and kissed us and promised never to leave us again.

As the rhetoric against refugees, particularly Muslim refugees, escalated, I grappled with so much hate directed toward them, me, or us. I don't have an accent, and if I didn't cover my hair, one would never assume that I was born in a different country, was fluent in a foreign language, or followed a religion, unlike most of my fellow citizens.

Chicago, USA 2016

In the fall of 2016, soon after school was back in session for my kids, I got a text from a friend of mine who is an ophthalmologist, Reema:

"I saw these people walking from the Extended Stay (affordable short and long-term hotels) by my home to the nearby grocery store. It was an older woman in a hijab and her husband. I stopped them to ask if they needed any help, but they only spoke Arabic, so I couldn't understand. I think they are new Syrian refugees. Do you think you could help translate for me?"

Out of the millions of Syrian refugees, 15,000 were resettled in the US in 2016. By 2017, that number dropped to 3000; in 2018, there were less than 100 Syrian refugees.

I agreed to meet Reema later that day at the Extended Stay, and we went and found them hanging out in the dining area. We found out that they were, in fact, newly arrived Syrian refugees. They had only been there for a few days and were waiting for the refugee agency to find them a place to live. They were there with their adult son, Musa, who was twenty-seven and was hit by a sniper bullet to his back. At first, they thought Musa would be paralyzed because he could not walk, but over time, he started to walk again with the help of a walker. Musa was married and left behind his wife and a ten-month-old daughter when they were granted refugee status in the US to seek further medical management for his bullet injury.

"Are you the only refugees here?" I asked.

"No. Another family arrived late yesterday evening. They are in room 2010," Musa's father told me.

"We should take them to dinner at Pita Inn," Reema said.

"That's a great idea. Who knows how long it's been since they have had a good Middle Eastern meal!" I replied.

I went to the second floor and knocked on the other family's room door. A beaming gentleman, Hazem, opened the door. He was in a wheelchair.

"Hello. My name is Nour, and I am from Homs, but I have lived my whole life in Chicago. Musa's family told me that you just arrived yesterday."

"Yes, it is me, my wife, and my two daughters," he said.

"We wanted to invite you for dinner tomorrow night to welcome you to Chicago."

"That is very kind of you."

"So, my husband and I and a few other friends will come to pick you up tomorrow at 6."

"Please, don't trouble yourselves."

"It's no trouble. We want to have a nice dinner and get to know you."

"Okay, we will be ready," he acquiesced.

"Great! See you tomorrow."

I called Amjad and told him about the two families on my way home.

"I invited them out to dinner tomorrow."

"Okay, sounds good."

"You have to come with me."

"Wait, what? What am I going to do? I won't be able to understand anything you guys say." My husband protested.

"I need your help. Two of the men are physically disabled, and I won't be able to get them in the car."

I knew he would agree. He has the biggest heart. He gets emotional watching videos of deployed military people surprising their children when they get home.

We all met the next day at the hotel at six. We learned about other families, so we invited them along. We took three cars, and Hazem ended up in the passenger seat next to me. It is a fifteen-minute drive to the restaurant, so I got to know Hazem a little during the drive. I told him I was a pediatric infectious diseases physician. He told me he used a wheelchair because he got polio as a child.

Upon hearing this, my instinct told me to feel sad for him. However, he was so cheerful and happy that he made it difficult for me to feel anything other than optimism.

He told me his daughters were three years old and nine months old. I told him that my family came to the United States when I was four and my sister was seven.

"They won't remember," I said.

"Won't remember what?"

"The trauma of being uprooted from their country of origin."

"I am relieved to hear you say that." He smiled.

"You can make a good life for them here. As difficult as it was for you and your wife to get here and as difficult as it will be over the next few months to acclimate to a whole new culture, language, and way of living, the good thing is that your daughters will not remember."

It's true. I don't remember anything from that time, nothing from the whole year we were separated from my father. However, suppose I close my eyes and think about it. In that case, a clear picture comes into my mind: my three-year-old self with my five-year-old sister sitting in the corner of a small balcony. I wore a red dress, and she wore a green one. Her hands were up, blocking the sun from her eyes. In a mushroom cut, my chestnut hair framed my tiny face with wire-rimmed glasses. Undoubtedly, my mom snapped that picture. On the back of it, I saw her familiar Arabic handwriting saying, "The girls on the balcony of our house in Homs." She had sent this picture by mail to my father during the year we were separated.

Did that little girl ever dream of being a physician in the United States, caring for some of the sickest American children? Like when I attained privileges at the community hospital where I currently work. The first baby I consulted was a former premature infant who had to have brain surgery for extra fluid around his brain. On the first day, I met the neonatologist, I insisted that something was wrong with the baby and that he needed an MRI.

"An MRI?"

"Yes, I think he has an abscess in his brain," I explained.

She looked at me with a puzzled facial expression. She was considerably older than I, and this was the first time she had met me.

"Why isn't he breathing over the vent?" I asked her.

No answer.

"He didn't have lung disease before the surgery, right?" I pressed on.

"Yes, that's right."

I don't blame her for not trusting me. An MRI is a lengthy procedure for an intubated neonate. My baby face also did not help. For all she knew, I graduated fellowship yesterday.

"Listen, his labs aren't back to normal, and he isn't acting right. I think he has an abscess. Please get the MRI." I pleaded with her.

As a consultant, I could only make my recommendations. I did not make the final decisions. I had earned my reputation at the hospital where I had worked for a long time, but this lady did not know me from any other medical student. Somehow, my pleading had convinced her.

Imagine my relief when later that night, I got a text from her as I set dinner for my family.

"I wanted to let you know that you were right. The neurosurgeon just evacuated 15 ccs of pus from that baby's ventricle. We sent it for culture." This is a standard procedure to see if bacteria grow from the evacuated pus.

"Great, I will follow up on the micro," I replied.

"You saved his life. Thank you." She concluded.

That was not the first time I had had this experience where I had been doubted but succeeded in convincing a person of higher rank within the medical field. One time, I consulted a ten-year-old boy on a Friday night. He had seen multiple physicians who had all thought he had pneumonia. He was being treated in the pediatric intensive care unit (PICU) with antibiotics. The intensivist called me because she wanted me to recommend which antibiotics he should be on since he had already been tried on three different ones and was not getting better. He had been seen by his primary care physician, a physician's partner, the ER physician, the admitting pediatric hospitalist, the pediatric intensivist, the pediatric surgeon, and the interventional radiologist. Everyone thought he had terrible pneumonia that was causing fluid around his lung, so he had a chest tube placed. They were waiting for me to make antibiotic recommendations. I sifted through his chart with multiple visits to physicians over three weeks and images of his chest.

Something did not add up. I finally turned to the PICU nurse said, "I don't think he has regular bacterial pneumonia. He either has tuberculosis or a lymphoma [cancer]."

Since it was already late in the evening and he was stable, I ordered a chest CT for the following day. A new ICU doctor was taking over for the weekend. She had the nurses send me a text thanking me for finally diagnosing him. He had cancer. I was sad for him and his family but relieved that he would finally get the proper treatment.

One can become arrogant if one believes in words like, "You saved his life." My faith keeps me grounded. I don't honestly believe I saved anyone's life. I think God intends for some people to live longer than others, and I am just a vehicle in this Master Plan. I believe that God gives talent and resources and can take them away within a blink of an eye. No one knows more than a doctor who sees the results of a traumatic brain injury (think car accident) for a CEO of a multi-million-dollar company.

I think about that little girl in the red dress a lot. I think about how strong my parents had to be to go through their struggles that year. Did my dad think he was ever going to see his family again? Did my mom worry about what was in store for her and her daughters in a new country?

I think about the person who finally stamped my passport with the visa. Did they think about who this little girl would grow up to become? Did they think about how she would contribute to the fabric of America?

Should it matter that I became a physician? I don't think so. Everyone has something to contribute. If I could not employ someone to help me with child care, I could not do what I do. I am very mindful of that fact. If I could not pick up a prepared meal from the restaurant down the street, I could not do what I do. If someone thinks he works in a silo, he is deluded.

When we finally got to the restaurant, we Americans split up, and each one or two of us sat with a newly-arrived family. My husband sat with our children, fed them, and entertained them. I sat with Hazem and his wife, Amani. She was shy at first but then opened up to me.

Amani started. "Hazem had his cell phone store in Aleppo, but it got bombed. Then, our neighbor's house also got bombed, which was the last straw for us." They left for Turkey with Hazem's mom, brother, and sister.

"We filled out the paperwork to try to come to the United States but didn't believe it would ever happen. After years of interviews [and the vetting process], we were finally chosen. We couldn't believe it." Hazem continued with a smile. "We felt so lucky."

Hazem's mom and sister were chosen too, but because Hazem's brother was not, his mom and sister stayed behind. Hazem, Amani, and their two daughters set out on this challenging journey hoping for a better life.

"Of course, we were scared and apprehensive, not sure if we made the right decision," Amani said. Her eyebrows furrowed.

I noticed that her baby was coughing a lot.

"Is your baby sick?" I asked her.

"Nour is a doctor," Hazem informed his wife.

"Yes, she has been coughing since we got on the plane in Turkey. She also feels warm," Amani said.

"Is she drinking okay?" I asked.

"Yeah, she is still drinking well."

"Is she still playing?" This sounds like a silly question, but once a child stops playing, that is a red flag in pediatric medicine.

"Yes, she is still playing."

"Maybe, she just has a cold virus," I said. "I will bring you some medicine to keep her temperature down."

After we dropped them off at the hotel, I quickly stopped at

Walgreens and got her some ibuprofen. I dropped it back to their room and promised to bring my stethoscope the next day to listen to her lungs. In the meantime, I gave them my number and told them to call me whenever they needed anything.

The next day was a Sunday, and I planned to see patients at the hospital. I stopped by the hotel as it was on my way to work. I listened to their baby and ascertained that she had bronchiolitis, an infection of the small airways. She looked like she was having trouble breathing. I told Amani and Hazem that their baby needed to go to the emergency room to ensure her breathing was okay. They were troubled by this news, but they trusted me. Amani got her diaper bag and the car seat the refugee agency had provided them with, and she came with me.

As we were heading downstairs, it dawned upon me that I was leaving a man paralyzed from the waist down with his three-year-old daughter in a hotel room in a country he had just arrived to where he did not speak one word of English. Three-year-olds can be challenging, especially when they have tantrums.

I knocked on Musa's family's hotel room, and the dad opened the door.

"Good morning. Sorry to bother you so early, but could you do me a favor and check up on Hazem every once in a while? I am taking his wife to the hospital because their baby is sick, and we are leaving him alone with his three-year-old daughter." He was happy to oblige, and although it was nowhere near ideal, it had to do for the time being.

We got to the ER, and it was a couple of hours wait. I did not have that much time because I was expected to see patients soon. I texted a friend who did not know Amani, but she agreed to stay with her and the baby while I went to work and back.

I don't think I am the exception to the typical human experience. I think I am the rule. It is easy to see yourself in someone else, I believe. I can imagine how difficult it could be for a mom of two young children to be uprooted from her country for the first time by barrel bombs to a country where everything was alien to her. Then, the mom is uprooted to yet another foreign country to give her daughters a chance at a better life. Although I don't remember any details of when my family first moved to Chicago, I don't actually have to remember. I envision it during my dialogue with the refugees. It is difficult to allow oneself not to see another from the "other" category, where it becomes easy to dehumanize and belittle them, to make them inconsequential and not deserving of a life of dignity and compassion.

The baby's chest X-ray confirmed the diagnosis of bronchiolitis. Still, her oxygen saturation was adequate to be released home, and within a few days, she recovered from her illness.

I continued visiting Hazem and Amani over the next year as they settled into their new apartment on Sheridan Drive, overlooking Lake Michigan. Despite the apartment being old and small, they had a beautiful view of the lake. When I visited, I brought something small for the girls and some food for the family. I helped them sort out and translate their mail. I helped them look around for a school for their eldest daughter. I gave them ideas of how Amani could earn an income. I watched them progress over the next year. They started taking English classes and enrolled their eldest in school and the youngest in daycare while they took their lessons. They learned how to navigate the transportation system of the city. They told me how friendly Chicagoans were.

Amani and Hazem were always happy to see me. They shared their hospitality, from Turkish coffee to the best desserts. They offered me their best. They also are not the exception; they are the rule. In every refugee tent I visited, I was invited to sit down and have something to drink or eat. These people, who had lost everything, were the most hospitable, open, and welcoming people. It makes me wonder if we could or would be just as generous in such humbled settings.

CHAPTER TEN

The Defeat

As the fall proceeded and the 2016 presidential campaign became heated, the candidate, Trump, amplified the anti-immigrant rhetoric, "We have some bad hombres here, and we are going to get them out," he said.

There is no way a guy who just said "bad hombres" on national television is getting elected. I was proven wrong.

One day that late fall, I was coming home after caring for a three-month-old baby named Carrie, who acquired late onset GBBS (group B beta-hemolytic streptococcus) sepsis and meningitis. Pregnant women are screened for this infection near the time of delivery. Suppose the mom is a carrier of the organism. In that case, she is usually treated with antibiotics before the baby's delivery to prevent the baby from acquiring the infection. Sometimes, moms can be negative, and the baby can still get the disease. That was the case here. I was preparing to have a heart-breaking conversation with the mom of this beautiful, precious baby girl. I had to tell her I was not sure her baby would ever walk, talk or hear. She only asked one question. "Will my baby see?" I am sure she asked me this because she noticed how we all have been checking her baby's pupillary reflexes every day, shining a light in her eyes to see how her pupils reacted.

"I don't know," I replied.

I always like to leave families with something hopeful. I knew I had to wrap it up, or my floodgates would open.

"Every child is different in how they recover from these things, and it's up to you to help your baby to live up to her fullest potential," I concluded.

Is that even fair? I thought to myself. To put all this pressure on the mom? Alternatively, maybe I had just said something that would stick with her forever through every physical therapy and occupational therapy appointment, her daughter's schooling, and beyond. Still, was that a good or bad move on my part?

Later that day, the baby had an MRI of her brain. As I logged on to the hospital's electronic medical record system to read her brain MRI results, I could only cry for half an hour. Uncontrollable sobbing.

It is as if I had just witnessed the moment in this woman's life when her life had changed forever. I watched this story unfold slowly before my eyes. This experience was where she was just postpartum and could clearly remember the happy hormones associated with having had a baby. What was also unforgettable were the heightened emotions a woman feels immediately postpartum. I could not bear thinking of how she would process this information from me.

I was not used to these kinds of cases. As a pediatric infectious diseases specialist, I relish that, in most cases, I can say to parents and kids as I discharge them from my clinic, "Your body is free of this infection now. I hope I never have to see you again; I know the feeling is mutual, and I am not offended." I would smile and say goodbye.

As I was driving home that day and still thinking about this family, the tears streamed down my face, forcing me to take my glasses off many times to wipe my eyes. I told myself that sometimes bad things happen to my patients, which affects me.

However, in 2016, what was new was that I suddenly became fully aware that I was a visibly Muslim woman in the current political climate. I was in my car, crying my head off for a reason that most human beings would completely understand. Instead of being fully able to focus on healing my broken heart, I had these fleeting, distracting thoughts like, *does that truck driver think I am crying because I am oppressed (see a scarf on my head) or does the lady in the car next to me think I am contemplating something horrendous like leaving an abusive spouse.*

I tried to shut those thoughts out because I knew I did not care what the truck driver was thinking and that I was just broken-hearted about my patient and her mom. But still. Part of me was angry that I *was* having these thoughts. I was not mad at myself because I recognized that I was experiencing normal human emotions. Thousands of other Muslim Americans had difficulty processing and navigating the current political climate. I was angry because I knew if the lady in the next lane's baby were in the ICU and knew who I was and what I did for a living, she would not care about my religious or ethnic background.

I decided to channel my anger about the rhetoric into writing an opinion piece I submitted to *USA Today*. The editor titled it, "Trump wants to lock out people like me." In this article, I described a typical day when I chose antibiotics to help save a child's life. When I was hired at my current job, my employer did not seem to care what my ethnic or religious background was. I did not care, nor have I ever cared, what religion, ethnic background, or immigration status my patients had. I am a refugee who grew up to become one of the most specialized physicians in the country, one of 1,500 pediatric infectious disease specialists, and one physician per 50,000 children.

In general, it has been my experience as a Muslim physician in the United States that my patients and their parents do not care about my religious background. However, some people do care what their doctor's religion, race, or ethnic background is and will request a different physician based on these criteria. I have not done a scientific study to gather the data on this, but I have read anecdotes of these experiences from the 150,000-member physician moms' Facebook group I belong to.

In March 2019, Lynne Shand, a councilor of a borough of Montreal named Anjou, took to social media to describe her frustration at having to be treated for a medical emergency by a veiled ophthalmologist. I wonder if Shand asked the doctor why she wore a head covering. Perhaps, she was not a Muslim after all. Perhaps, she was a cancer survivor who hid her bald head after her hair had fallen out due to chemotherapy. Alternatively, maybe, she was wearing the head covering as a sign of solidarity with the Muslims of Christchurch, New Zealand, where a terrorist walked into two mosques and shot dead 51 unarmed worshippers. Regardless, Shand was upset because she could not refuse this doctor's assistance. I suppose she could have suffered the ramifications of her medical emergency. I wonder how she would have felt if the ophthalmologist had refused to treat a racist. I have never met a Muslim doctor who refused to treat a patient, but they could exist. Shand explicitly said she was not a racist. *The lady doth protest too much, methinks.*

After my opinion piece was published in *USA Today*, it spread like wildfire among my friends and their networks on social media. I wondered why I needed to justify my existence with my ability to help save someone's child's life. My existence should matter whether I can help play a small role in saving a life or not. Thousands of people walk thousands of miles across Europe or Central America through Mexico toward the US border. Those people should matter, and as Donald Trump was eventually elected as the President of the USA, I realized that maybe we do not matter. I felt defeated at the time, but perhaps, not discouraged.

CHAPTER ELEVEN

The Surprise

Chicago, USA 2017

"If we can't get a regular flight into Yemen, we can get you guys on a UN private chartered jet that can pick you up from any private airport either in Egypt or Jordan and fly you into Aden. Or another option is a private WHO jet. That will cost about $45,000. I am negotiating for $25,000."

That was the next set of texts sent from the on-the-ground contact, Mahmood, on our WhatsApp group entitled, "Medical mission to Yemen" in the summer of 2017.

This mission had been in the works since the beginning of 2017. Yemen had already been plunged into its third year of conflict, which started when a Houthi rebel movement tried to seize government control. In 2015, the conflict escalated when Coalition forces consisting of multiple Arab states led by Saudi Arabia and backed by the US and the UK began airstrikes.[5] We had applied for and got issued visas, only to have them expire before we could secure flights because of airport closings and bombings. We applied again. We sent our passports to the Yemeni embassy in Washington, DC. During the second application round, the embassy held my passport back for no clear reason. *Divine intervention? Maybe I am not meant to go. Perhaps I should not be going.* "Even Yemenis aren't going to Yemen!" My husband tried to reason with me.

I continued to pray the *istikharah* prayer, which is supposed to guide a Muslim one way or the other. After multiple phone calls to the embassy and days off with the embassy being closed and many "*insha'Allah*" (Arabic for God-willing), my passport finally arrived.

It was then the end of August. I had some planned time off in

September, plus my three kids, aged eight, six, and three, would be in school by September. The original plan was to go sometime in the summer, but I did not want to leave while my kids were off and certainly did not want to leave my husband with three young children at home all day. I made a special request that the trip to Yemen be delayed until the end of September. By then, the two older kids would have acclimated to returning to school, and my youngest son, Zaid, hopefully, I prayed, would have adjusted to starting school. After all, he wanted to be like his big brother, Hamza, and his big sister, Aya. He was so excited about his Dusty Crophopper backpack with the movable propeller. He was very social, so I thought he would adjust.

Zaid was so easy-going. He was my easiest baby: a good sleeper, a good eater, was not fussy, and did not experience colic. It was an easy transition for my husband and me, who had gone from a family of four to a family of five. However, I wanted a fourth baby so badly. Coming from a small family myself, I could not help it. I wanted my children to have multiple siblings to share life's ups and downs and create an extensive support system. By the summer of 2017, my husband and I had been trying to conceive a fourth child for nearly two years. It was not working.

I turned 40 that summer, and my youngest child would start preschool in the fall. I began to come to terms with the fact that four children may not have been meant for us and, perhaps, not ideal. I envisioned a glimmer of more free time that would come back to me with having all three of my children in school. By that summer, I had given away all the baby items scattered throughout our home for the past eight years.

Imagine my shock a couple of weeks before we were supposed to fly out into a war zone when I realized my period was late. *No way! This CANNOT be happening. Not now, at least.* I did not even have a pregnancy test at home. The next day on my way home from work, I stopped at a Walgreens and picked one up, went home, and took the test. It was positive. *Now what?*

Indeed, if I told the team leader, there was no way he was going to take a pregnant woman into a war zone. I did not have to think about it or make any decisions. He was not just going to say, "No," he was also going to say a resounding "Absolutely not!" I first sent a text hinting that I had a change of plans.

"I see there is a total of five doctors still on the WhatsApp group planning to take this trip."

"No, the fifth guy backed out; it's still just the four of us," Zaher immediately replied.

By then, the many out-of-this-world possibilities of how we would get to Yemen had been finally narrowed down to a practical one: flying to Cairo via Istanbul and then boarding a Yemenia Airways flight directly into Aden. Over the past couple of months, the airline was sometimes functional. The airports in Yemen were occasionally open and sometimes not.

"Have the airline tickets been purchased? If not, don't buy mine before we talk," I instructed.

"Sounds like you are trying to back out," Zaher replied.

"I have new circumstances," I said.

"We changed the dates of the mission for you."

Way to lay it on thick, Zaher.

"Just call me," I surrendered.

"I am in Geneva. I will call you in a bit."

At that point, I still had not told my husband. The one who had spent the last few weeks reminding me how Yemenis were not even traveling to Yemen. There was no way the conversation was going to go: "Guess what. I am pregnant!" and him replying, "What better way to celebrate than by you traveling into a war zone!"

Maybe I was not the best judge of what pregnant women should and should not do. Thankfully, I had experienced relatively easy pregnancies up to that point. I worked until the last day of each of my pregnancies. I remained quite active as a pediatric hospitalist at an extensive tertiary care teaching hospital for the first two pregnancies and at a referral women and children's hospital in the suburbs of Chicago for my third pregnancy. Being a hospitalist requires a lot of energy.

I also remained physically active outside of the job. For example, when I was pregnant with my second child, my daughter, Aya, it was unseasonably warm one October day in Michigan. I was 36 weeks pregnant, and my husband had borrowed a jet ski from one of his friends and wanted to go jet skiing. Not one to pass up an adventure, I decided to go with him. As an avid swimmer, I would not pass up the opportunity, knowing what lay ahead in caring for a newborn. I had a blast in the water.

During the second trimester of my third pregnancy, I traveled to Saudi Arabia to perform the Lesser Pilgrimage (*umrah*), taking along my then five-year-old and three-year-old. That is a physically grueling endeavor as it is usually quite crowded in Mecca during the Lesser Pilgrimage. Think thousands and thousands of people! The religious act entails a roughly four-mile walk amidst a sea of people.

Having had these experiences in mind, I felt like I knew my body well enough to guesstimate that I could probably handle the grueling medical mission experience physically. It isn't like this was my first mission, either. I knew from previous experience that to be successful on a medical mission, one needed to be flexible, think and act fast, work with limited resources, and be creative and patient. Things did not always happen as planned. The efficiency in transportation services we were used to in the United States was usually unavailable in the Middle East. The hierarchy of the business models that we were accustomed to, where the customer is always right and if there is something wrong, one took it up with management, hardly existed in areas where medical missions were undertaken. I knew how to improvise and was confident in coping with another mission's challenges.

Chicago, USA 2017

During the planning phases, we received a text from Mahmood, whom we had never met before, but who would handle the logistics: "How much sleep do you need? How much time does it take you to eat and shower? Do you need a certain water temperature to shower? Any food restrictions or allergies?"

The questions caught me off guard. *What kind of doctors was Mahmood used to working with?* It seemed from the line of questions he asked that, perhaps, he had worked with some entitled ones. He confirmed that later in the trip, but I knew we would not be like any group he had worked with. We were seasoned and were not expecting the five-star treatment. We were going to one of the poorest countries in the Middle East that had been caught up in a war. To expect anything besides the bare minimum would have been foolish and selfish.

"Hello?" I answered the phone call from Zaher.

"*Salaam,* Nour. How are you?"

"*Wa alaykum assalaam.* I am good. How about yourself?" I replied.

"I am good. So tell me. What's up? What are your new circumstances?" He did not waste any time.

"I am pregnant. It is a total surprise!"

"Wow, congratulations!" I could hear in his voice that he was smiling. "I am so happy for you guys. That's great news."

"Thank you. So this explains why I was telling you not to buy my ticket."

"Oh. I see. So you are not going to come?" He sounded surprised.

"I mean. I didn't think you would want to take a pregnant woman. I don't want to slow you guys down."

"How many weeks are you?"

"Around six. It's very early."

"And how do you feel?" He inquired.

"I mean. I have pretty easy pregnancies. Thank God. I get some morning sickness, but I don't vomit or anything. I usually work right up until the end."

"Well. What did Amjad say?" He asked about my husband's reaction.

"I haven't told him yet. I just took the test." *Because I thought you would say NO!*

He laughed. "Oh. Well, I don't want to pressure you. But you know, you would be the only woman on the mission. I think you would give a different perspective and hear different things about the situation in Yemen from the female population. Plus, you are an infectious diseases expert and a pediatrician. I think you would be highly valuable to our team. I don't know. Think about it. I would understand if you didn't want to come."

"I really do want to come. I don't know. I have to talk with my husband and think about it."

"Okay. Well, let me know. We must buy the plane tickets within the next couple of days."

"Okay. I will text you."

"Okay. Congratulations again!"

"Thanks!"

I was surprised by the direction that the conversation took. I thought I would be off the hook about deciding whether I should travel to a country engulfed in a war where children tend to be the most significant casualties. Had Zaher declined to take me, I would have been absolved of responsibility. However, I could not unlearn what I knew about the situation in Yemen, and I knew I could help, even in a small way.

Like many middle-aged working American mothers, I had reached a place where I was starting to feel I was losing myself. I was slowly feeling pieces of my identity slipping away and being replaced by the mindless, automated responsibilities of keeping a household running. Of course, teaching my children how to be dignified human beings on this Earth is never mindless, but when children are very young, those meaningful conversations are few and far between. Most of my day outside work was spent changing diapers, cooking meals, loading the dishwasher, loading the washer, emptying the dryer, folding and putting away clothes, and cleaning up in the kitchen. Yes, there are beautiful moments of irreplaceable joy snuggling up with a child before bed or delighting in the music of uncontrollable giggles during tickle wars.

Nevertheless, there was always a risk that far more prevalent energy-consuming daily tasks would drown out those experiences. Although my husband helped when asked to, I was tired of asking about things that were blatantly obvious and necessary to keep our household going. Like most couples, we had been through the peaks and valleys of marriage and were in a canyon during that particular time.

After I hung up with Zaher, I went to the basement where Amjad worked in the home office. I knocked on the door.

"Come in."

I took a seat on the other side of his desk.

"My period was late this week. So, I just took a pregnancy test." The mood between us was somber. All our unspoken issues were looming.

"And?" He was shocked.

"I am pregnant." I could not help but smile because I had wanted this baby for so long, but I was trying not to smile because I had so much pent-up resentment toward him.

"Oh. Wow." I knew he did not know how to react. He did not know if I was happy because he knew I had wanted this baby for so long or upset because... After all, I had finally come to terms with not having a baby and started to talk about the fact that with Zaid going to school in the fall, I might be able to get back to the gym more regularly and take care of my health. And then, of course, there was the looming trip to Yemen that he had already expressed concern about.

"So, what does that mean? You're not going to go to Yemen anymore, are you?"

"I don't know."

"What do you mean you don't know?" He pressed on.

"I mean, I don't know. If I don't go on this trip now, that's it for me. I am not going anywhere for at least another two years!"

I didn't have to explain to him how much I benefited from these trips on both emotional and spiritual levels, how I felt that I got back so much more than I gave.

"I don't think Zaher will take a pregnant woman."

"He said he would take me if I wanted to go. I already told him and told him I was going to discuss it with you first."

"Well, you already know how I feel about this trip. Your being pregnant makes my opinion stronger. But I know you. You are going to do whatever you are going to do."

"I am going to keep praying *istikhara*."

As I had already done the *istikhara* prayer before knowing I was pregnant, I needed to do it again in my new circumstances, asking God whether going to Yemen in my current situation was the right thing to do. The prayer starts by acknowledging God's Infinite Knowledge and Power. Then, one proceeds to ask God: "If such and such a matter is good for me in my faith, my life, and my Hereafter, make it easy for me and put blessings for me in this endeavor. And, if You know that it is bad for me in my faith, life or Hereafter, then divert me from it and divert it from me, bless me with what is meant for me and make me content with what You have decreed." It is compelling because it leaves me ultimately feeling at peace with whatever the outcome is. I feel at ease believing that God would protect me from something, whether emotionally or spiritually, in the physical world.

I had one thing going for me: my husband's complete trust in me when I said I would make that prayer. He and I had always seen the wisdom behind any way our life turned out after I had made that prayer. So much so that any time we needed to make a big decision, whether it was buying a home, moving, or even buying a car, he turned to me and said, "Can you pray [the] *istikhara* [prayer], please?" Even though he was perfectly capable of praying it himself.

For the next few days, I prayed the *istikhara* prayer multiple times a day and asked God to help me make the right decision. I decided to text my best friend, Ingrid, seeking some advice. I was not completely forthcoming about my current new state. However, I had told her I signed up for a medical mission to Yemen and was getting scared because of the military situation. Ingrid had worked as a midwife in a war zone in the early 1980s. She was no stranger to administering humanitarian aid in dangerous situations.

"If you don't have full confidence in your team, especially the team leader, that he would not put you in a dangerous situation, pull out and offer a monetary donation," she advised.

"I trust them fully," I replied.

"Then, I think you should go."

With that, I texted Zaher to buy my ticket. But I continued to pray for guidance until I got on the plane.

CHAPTER TWELVE

Compartmentalization

Chicago, USA 2017

On that fateful September 8, 2017, we all met at O'Hare International Airport in Chicago. I said my goodbyes to my children and drove with my husband to the airport. Despite his sincere hesitations, he had come to terms with the fact that I was determined to make this trip.

Although the trip had been in the making for months, it had only come to reality one week before take-off. This was a blessing in disguise because once the tickets were purchased and reality set in, I am not going to lie; I was scared. Multiple times during that week, I intermittently started crying, wondering whether I was making a mistake, whether I was going to get killed on this trip and whether I was ever going to see my children again. When my husband caught me sobbing, he asked, "Then, why are you going?"

As I dropped the kids off, I wondered if these were the last days I would take them to school. I found my mind wandering to the future. If I did not make it back, who would be there to help any of my children when they ushered in a first child? Who could reassure them that those difficult sleepless nights of being a parent to a newborn would quickly pass and promise my child that life would get better? Who would be there to console a broken heart or celebrate a dream achieved? I countered these thoughts with, at least I have the luxury of having visions of my children's future. Do the moms in Yemen have these dreams? Or are they just wondering if their children will make it past the next few weeks or months? Are they just praying their children don't suffer shrapnel wounds, traumatic amputations, and devastating brain injuries?

I could not even articulate why I was so resolved to go on this trip. I knew Yemen was suffering from the worst humanitarian crisis of our time. The *New York Times* had just published an article in August 2017 entitled "'It's a Slow Death:' The World's Worst Humanitarian Crisis.[6]" Yemen was experiencing one of the world's most significant cholera outbreaks. This completely preventable infectious disease has the potential to cause death by dehydration due to the poor sanitation situation. Maybe it was cholera that roped me in. As an infectious diseases specialist, death by preventable contagious diseases haunted me.

Just a few years before, I followed the news closely as polio had been reported to be re-emerging in Syria due to the conflict. Syria had not seen a case of polio since 1999, but in October of 2013, two years into the crisis, the first case was reported. With the war continuing, as expected, vaccine rates in children dropped. It was horrifying to know that in addition to the suffering brought on by bombing campaigns that left hundreds of children maimed and injured, the Syrian children also had to risk acquiring a vaccine-preventable disease that would have devastating effects on the nervous system with resultant partial or complete paralysis. Unfathomable for a country being led by a medical doctor (the current president of Syria, Bashar al-Assad, is an ophthalmologist by training).

In addition to the cholera outbreak, Yemenis were suffering from malnutrition. In children, malnutrition causes stunted growth and development. A child who was already malnourished while infected with cholera has no reserve to rely on when facing massive amounts of diarrhea. As a pediatrician and as a mother, it devastated me. I am sure the raging hormones of early pregnancy did not help curb my emotional responses to these facts.

Then, there was the fact that I did not hear a lot from the Yemeni diaspora in the United States. As a Syrian-American, I thought the

Yemenis could learn from our experience. After all, the Syrian had passed its fourth anniversary when Coalition forces launched military campaign of airstrikes and bombings into Sana'a, Yemen's capital city.

I also believe that people we help pray for us. When I was 13 years old, my parents took my sister and me to Mecca on the Sacred Pilgrimage, *Hajj*. The journey impacted my life in many ways. I was surrounded by two million people of every race and ethnicity, speaking hundreds of different languages and from every socioeconomic background. One of the most significant events during that journey was one I often return to and think of as central to my religious beliefs. It was an act of mercy.

We had been walking for hours under the assaulting eastern Meccan heat. Since two million people were trying to go to the same place at the same time in a city of narrow streets, sometimes it was just faster (still hours on end) to walk rather than take a bus. It was June and over 100 degrees Fahrenheit. Thirty minutes into our walk, I ran out of water, so I was parched. At some point, the flow of human traffic was stopped, and I looked over to my right and saw a man in his 30s of African origin open his thermos of water and take a sip. He saw me looking at him. He saw my bright red face, the beads of sweat rolling off my dry, cracked lips. Then, he opened his Thermos and offered it to me. And I took the best gulp of water I ever had.

This man, whom I did not know had offered me, a young, thirsty girl, some of his water. I thanked him but never saw him again. I prayed for him, though, while I was at *Hajj* and every year around the time of *Hajj*. And I randomly remember him at other times of the year and pray for him again because he did not have to offer me any of his precious commodities. However, he did because he was a good, caring human being.

I believe these prayers protect the ones who did the good deed or their loved ones. For example, after I returned from Yemen and had my baby boy, Kareem, I believed a prayer of someone I helped in my mission protected him. I was coming home from the grocery store with him. He was in his infant car seat and had fallen asleep. I carried him in with six bags of groceries because, God forbid, I would have to make another trip out to the car (*if you know, you know*). I put the groceries and the car seat down on our concrete steps and tried to unlock the door. I must have put the car seat too close to the edge because as soon as I opened the door, his little car seat tumbled down three concrete steps onto the concrete driveway. Of course, he woke up and wailed. My heart plummeted as I ran down the steps to get him. However, he had no scratch when I turned the car seat over. Yes, I know those things are built to protect, but I think it also could have been way worse, and I remember thinking to myself, somebody must have prayed for me today.

Every time I started to worry about the trip to Yemen, I reminded myself that I had complete confidence in the two senior physicians I would travel with. Both were long-time veterans of medical missions and had recently been named "Chicagoans of the Year in 2016" for traveling to Aleppo, Syria, in June of 2016, amidst fierce bombardment, to work in the last remaining hospital in the largest city in Syria, which was operating covertly. Every day, I renewed my intention, commitment, and resolve to travel to Yemen, but that did not erase the fear.

As a physician, I am very well-trained to compartmentalize my feelings, especially as a pediatric subspecialist. There is no way I could function in my job on some days if I did not acquire that skill early on in my training days. In adult medicine, when a patient dies, sometimes they have lived a long, full life, and sometimes they and their family members have already made peace with the fact that the patient may never leave the hospital. That is never the case in pediatrics. When a child dies, even if it was expected, it is devastating, heartbreaking, and just plain awful. There are no words to describe how healthcare workers, especially mothers, feel when a child dies unexpectedly.

One never knows which patient will hit you the hardest or why. I have had a few deaths of children during my years of practice. Thankfully, they have been few and far between. My first one happened during my first week as a second-year resident in my first intensive care unit rotation. We were only required to do two ICU rotations during residency. I chose an extra month as an elective. I liked the rotation because I learned a lot, but I did not think I had the emotional stamina to handle pediatric deaths in the long run.

Chicago, USA 2004

My first experience with the death of a pediatric patient happened when an eight-year-old boy with a chronic illness, Kevin, ended up in our ICU that July. His mother had made the heartbreaking decision to make him DNR (do not resuscitate). This was an expected death. He had kidney failure, developmental delays, and was nonverbal. She had decided no more dialysis for him. My attending physician explained that his potassium would rise if not dialyzed off, which would eventually cause his heart to stop. The process would happen over a couple of days.

Pediatric ICU nurses are the best. They protect their patients, so sometimes, they can be harsh on residents. The nurses did everything they could to make Kevin and his mom comfortable. They even brought in a little radio that played in his room. His mom snuggled in bed with him every night. She sang to him and caressed his hair. As I signed out to the on-call resident the day before he died, I stopped by his room on my way out. He and his mom were taking a nap. They were cuddled together in the bed as rays of afternoon sun flooded through the window. The radio was playing "My Immortal" by Evanescence.

I'm so tired of being here
Suppressed by all my childish fears
And if you have to leave
I wish that you would just leave
Cause your presence still lingers here
And it won't leave me alone
These wounds won't seem to heal; this pain is just too real
There's just too much that time cannot erase
When you cried, I'd wipe away of your tears
When you'd scream, I'd fight away all of your fears
And I held your hand through all of these years
But you still have all of me.

I stood in the doorway, watching them and listening to the words, tears streaming down my face. By the following day, he died. It is funny how memory works. How these moments are associated with a song or a scent and that no matter where life takes you, that song or smell can immediately take you back ten or fifteen years, bringing all those emotions flooding back!

When I came for rounds the next day, I saw that all the machines attached to Kevin were turned off. There was a calm silence in his room. My co-resident informed me that he had passed early in the morning. One of the things that shocked me the most was the nurses and the attending physician running around getting work done, just moving on.

"How can you all just move on like that?" I managed through tears to my stoic attending with the statuesque face and long brown-haired braids. She had pulled me into her office.

"Nour, you should take some time to get yourself together. Go wash your face and come back and join us for rounds when you are ready," she said.

"What do you mean? You act like a human being did not just die?!" I was young and judgmental.

"A human being did die, but I have a lot of other patients who need me right now, and it would not serve them well if I just broke down and cried. So take the time you need and return when ready."

I was not a mother back then. I can say, though, since having children, having a pediatric patient die now is a thousand times worse. As I mentioned earlier, when I trained to be a doctor, taking care of my mental health was not something we discussed. After a pediatric patient dies, there are debriefs where people can discuss how they feel and why they think it is hitting them so hard. The phenomenon of how a healthcare worker is affected by a patient's death is real, whether the healthcare worker is a doctor, nurse, child-life specialist, clinical coordinator, or social worker. It is natural. When the patient is at their sickest, we are all on auto-pilot, holding back all emotions, almost holding our breath. It is not until after the time of death is called, all the family members have said their goodbyes and left the hospital, and the deceased's body is removed from the room that we all can breathe again. And then, watch out because the flood of emotions will knock us over.

Chicago, USA 2018

Grief is an interesting phenomenon. It comes in waves, and when you think you are done grieving, it knocks you over again. In December 2018, one of my patients, who was a four-month-old infant, died unexpectedly. He physically reminded me of my baby, a few months older than him. It was around winter break, so my children were off from school, and they witnessed me intermittently crying. I tried to be as honest as I could with my children without scaring them. That is what child psychologists teach us to do. If we are not honest with our children, they make up scenarios worse than the actual situation. Over winter break, I took my kids to Winter Wonderfest at Navy Pier. It was an annual tradition. We ice skate there, decorate cookies, ride the carnival rides and jump around in the bouncy houses. When I look back at some of the pictures I took with my kids there, I see my face smiling, but my eyes convey a different reality. A person's eyes can honestly give it all away.

Ann Arbor, USA 2004

Don't get me wrong. It's not all sad in pediatrics. It's mostly happy. Most kids fight off illness very well. They are resilient, which is one of the things that drew me to the field. I remember when I was a fellow in Ann Arbor, we saw a teenage boy who had a very aggressive MRSA (methicillin-resistant Staphylococcus aureus) lung infection. It destroyed a little over one-half of one of his lungs. He was so sick that he had to go on ECMO (extracorporeal membrane oxygenation) for several weeks. A heart-lung bypass machine that takes all of your blood out of your body, oxygenates it, and then puts it back in your body. In the medical world, that is throwing the kitchen sink at a patient; a last-ditch effort before you think your patient will die. A couple of months later, I had to do a double take because he was walking around as if nothing had ever happened to him. I stopped to chat with him. Of course, he did not remember me because he was sedated while on this machine. He told me he was back to playing football without half a lung. What could I say other than, "Go Blue!"

Chicago, USA 2017

Thus, I tried to remember the art of compartmentalization as my husband drove our unborn child and me to the airport on my humanitarian mission to Yemen. I tried to remember for his sake, for my children's sake, and for the sake of all the children I would soon treat in a country where rejoining a football team was a luxury they could not afford. I pray for them and wonder if they pray for me, too, sometimes.

CHAPTER THIRTEEN

The Other

Chicago, USA 2017

At the airport, the four-physician team met. It was me, a pediatric infectious diseases specialist; John, a retired pediatrician; Zaher, a pulmonary and critical care specialist; and Faiz, an internal medicine physician who had just graduated residency. We were four generations of physicians.

This trip would be the maiden medical mission for the newly formed NGO, MedGlobal. When we first traveled to Hatay, Turkey, in September 2011, Zaher was president of the Syrian-American Medical Society (SAMS). It was primarily a social organization for Syrian-American physicians that held some CME (continuing medical education) activities and social gatherings. They had just started holding CME conferences in the capital of Syria, Damascus (before the civil unrest began), and were training Syrian physicians. SAMS had an annual budget of under $100,000 and one part-time employee.

After our trip to Turkey, SAMS, under the leadership of Zaher, became an internationally recognized medical NGO with a budget in the millions and employees on three different continents over four years. After years spent focusing on the Syrian crisis, Zaher eventually joined forces with John Kahler, a veteran humanitarian pediatrician, and Anu Shivaraju, another veteran of medical missions and interventional cardiologist, to form MedGlobal. He invited me to serve on the Board of Directors, and going to Yemen would be the first medical mission for this young organization.

Given the gravity of our trip, we were the last ones to check-in. Additionally, Zaher, our team leader and the most veteran traveler among us, forgot his passport at home. The ticket agents kept telling us they could not wait for his passport. If a particular time came and his passport was not present, he could not board. I don't think I would have boarded the flight without him. He had established contact with the partnering local NGO that was going to be responsible for our safety and security.

Maybe I am not meant to go on this trip, after all, I thought to myself. Amjad tried his best to sweet-talk the agents. One of the many things I appreciate about my husband is that even though he did not think I should go, once he understood that I had resolved to go, he did everything in his power to support me and facilitate my trip. Amjad told the agents about the medical missions Zaher had attended previously, how many lives he had affected, and how we were not just going on some leisurely trip to Cairo. By some great miracle, he kept them talking and the check-in process was open until Zaher's passport arrived. The trip was on.

Thankfully, I slept most of the ten-hour flight to Istanbul. At Istanbul airport, we met our facilitator from the partnering NGO, Mahmood. He was a fast-talking, get-things-done kind of guy. He updated us that fighting had broken out in Aden, which was our intended destination. "It's too dangerous to fly into Aden," he said. "I am arranging for us to fly into Sey'oun, and from there, we will go to Ma'rib." Zaher turned to me and asked. "Where is Sey'oun?"

"How am I supposed to know? Aren't you the one who grew up in the Middle East?" When we got to Cairo, we had plenty of time to look it up.

Faiz did not hesitate to do a Google search of "Ma'rib." He showed me a Wikipedia page that he had found on his phone. It said Ma'rib was an ISIS strong-hold. It is funny how the human brain functions. Although I, like most of my fellow Americans, had seen and heard the news of all of the grotesque things that ISIS had done to many of its captors, all I kept thinking was, *I hope I don't get cholera*. I think it was because I had experienced food poisoning and how awful it felt to vomit, suffer from diarrhea, and subsequent dehydration and lethargy. Those were tangible experiences for me. Being captured and tortured by ISIS was something my mind could not fully grasp. I tried to let that fact about Ma'rib come in one ear and out the other.

Regardless, I could not help but think about the Jordanian fighter pilot Muath al-Kasasbeh, who had been captured by ISIS in December 2014 and burned alive in early 2015, the horrific act videotaped for the world to witness. Al-Kasasbeh had been a member of a prominent Sunni Muslim family in Jordan. He was piloting a fighter jet involved in a military intervention against ISIS. I also thought of Peter Kassig, the young 26-year-old humanitarian aid worker delivering food and medical supplies to Syrians in need when ISIS captured him in October 2013. While in captivity, Peter converted to Islam, something he had been contemplating long before his capture. But that did not matter. The fact that he was also a humanitarian aid worker and not a soldier did not matter. He was tortured and beheaded by ISIS one year later. That was enough evidence for me that my religious affiliation or my medical work would not be enough to protect me from being dehumanized and demonized as the "other."

What kind of savage burns a human being alive or beheads another human being? The same type who would walk in and shoot up worshipers at the Tree of Life Synagogue - eleven dead, seven injured; the Mother Emanuel Church - nine dead, three injured; Oak Creek Sikh Temple - six dead, four wounded; and Christchurch Mosque - 51 dead and dozens injured.

Hate is hate. It can be disguised in your religion or mine, your race or mine, your ethnic background or mine. It does not matter.

Being demonized as "the other" would not have been a new experience for me. I had spent a little over a decade before the attacks of 9/11 wearing the hijab. Before 2001, the experience had been somewhat innocuous. My fellow citizens perceived that I probably came from another country, spoke a different language, and perhaps did not understand English well.

Chicago, USA 1998

Sometimes, it was more than innocuous. Like when I was interviewing for medical school and one of the interviewers, a psychiatrist, was quite hateful and not afraid to show it. She asked me how I expected to become a physician, given my religious beliefs that there should be no physical contact between unrelated men and women. Even though I tried to explain to her, a woman twice my age and in a place of authority, how my religion allowed for exemptions in health matters, she plowed forward with the hateful rhetoric.

I must admit, I was disheartened. The interview made me question whether or not this was the right field for me. Nevertheless, I persisted. I had decided that I was not going to let her deter me. I had just spent the last four years of my life where "fun comes to die." That was one of the slogans printed on the back of the University of Chicago T-shirts sold in our bookstore. The university was competitive, and being pre-med was cut-throat competitive, as the students used to say. To say that I studied hard was an understatement. I did not have the luxury of graduating from an elite high school like some of my counterparts.

I had graduated from a new parochial all-girls high school located inside a mosque because there was not enough money for an actual building. My science lab was in the mosque's kitchen. That was where I learned how to dissect a frog. I will never forget my first year at the university. After fierce competition, I was always the first at the chemistry lab and the last to leave. I did not know how to put the lab equipment together. I had never seen a burette, let alone measured anything in it. I had never handled a condenser and did not know how to connect it.

Years after graduating, my sister told me, "Baba never thought you would make it."

Oh.

I had a Chinese TA (teacher's assistant), a chemistry graduate student. In his thick-rimmed black glasses and maroon vest, he tried his best to help me. I could tell he felt sorry for me. I was always at his office hours on Mondays, trying to get help with the problem sets. When I was utterly stressed before the final exam, he said, "Nour, just study. Don't eat. Don't sleep. Don't socialize. Just study!"

And that is precisely what I did. I left my dorm at 7:45 AM every morning to make it in time for my 8:00 AM classes. Classes ended around noon. I got home, ate lunch, prayed the mid-day prayer, and set off for the lab, where I remained from 1-5 PM. I prayed again at the dorm before heading off to the Crerar Science Library every night until it closed at 1:30 AM. Then, I would go home and get some sleep, only to start over again with the same routine the next day. People talk about the "freshman fifteen" (a belief that students gain 15 pounds during their first year of university). I lost the "freshman fifteen" because of the schedule I kept. However, it paid off, and I graduated in three years and one quarter with honors and a bachelor's degree in Cellular and Molecular Biology. I was not going to let this bigoted psychiatrist get in my way. Now, I am grateful that my 21-year-old self exercised so much resolve.

I was fuming when I got home from that interview with the lady who could not understand how my religion allowed me to work as a physician. I made an appointment with my pre-med student advisor, Daniel, a middle-aged white man. I welcomed the musty smell of old books and the built-in gothic bookshelves of his office.

"What happened?" He asked, peering in from behind his frameless lenses.

"She just kept asking me questions about my religion!"

"What?"

"Yes. That's so illegal. She violated my civil rights."

He nodded.

"I am going to write them a letter. She can't just do that to people," I proclaimed.

He agreed, but Daniel hesitated when he read my scathing letter.

"Maybe, you should tone it down a bit."

I knew he feared that medical school admissions committee members ran in small circles. He thought I would be black-balled.

The more one ascends the steps in academia, especially in the sciences, the more faith is looked down upon. It is considered a pacifying agent and something irrational. Regardless, that has not been my personal experience. My faith teaches me that if the whole world conspires to prevent me from something God has already destined for me, I will attain that. That understanding provides me with unparalleled courage. I sent that letter unchanged.

Three years after that eventful interview, the experience for Muslim Americans became so much worse. After the attacks on 9/11 in the United States, my religion became synonymous with the word "terrorism." Consequently, according to the Pew Research Center, hate crimes against Muslims rose seven-fold after 9/11. Anti-Muslim intimidation increased, as did vandalism. I was pretty used to being labeled as "the other" by fellow countryfolk.

Cairo, Egypt 2017

Upon our arrival in Cairo, we spent the day and night in an upscale hotel. We cleaned up and rested before we met at dinner time. At dinner, we talked about logistics. I could tell our whole team was a little on edge as we planned to catch a flight on the only airline flying into Yemen those days, Yemenia Airways. Faiz tried to watch a football game on his phone, which he shared with John. For the life of me, I still do not understand the details of American football. I could not share in their distraction. Zaher and Mahmood were discussing logistics. I tuned them out too. I tried to be present, listening to the lyrics of Fairuz, the famous Lebanese singer, blaring from the hotel restaurant.

During those days, Yemenia Airways only flew in and out of Sey'oun three times a week. The flight could not be booked online. Ticket purchases had to be done in person, in cash. We purchased our tickets, and we were on our way. I had a whole row to myself. After all, "even Yemenis were not traveling to Yemen." I walked around the nearly empty flight and saw my colleagues napping. I was on hyper-alert, and there was no way I was going to fall asleep on that flight.

CHAPTER FOURTEEN

The Military

When we left the United States for Yemen, the Yemenis suffered from relentless conflict for four years. OCHA (United Nations Office for the Coordination of Humanitarian Affairs) has estimated that about 20 million people need humanitarian aid. Just over half of the population, or 17 million people, were food insecure. Less than half of the health centers were functional, and no doctors were left in 49 of 276 districts.

Yemen 2017

When we landed in Sey'oun's small airport, a team of soldiers from Coalition forces descended upon us, all armed with AK-47s. They greeted us warmly and told us they would be our military escorts to our final destination, Ma'rib. They said they would take us to get cleaned up and have breakfast as our luggage, including four bags of medical supplies and medications, was being cleared by customs. They took us in armored vehicles. We rode in a caravan with a pick-up truck filled with soldiers in front of us and two trucks behind us, one of which had a weapon capable of striking down a helicopter.

We were taken to military barracks. They served us fried eggs and other traditional Middle-Eastern breakfast food like olives, *halawa*, olive oil, *za'atar*, and tea. Military barracks in the Middle East were filled with men. It was quite unheard of for a woman to be an active combatant soldier in the Middle East. So, I found myself surrounded by men. And this would become a recurring theme of the trip for me. I asked if I could use the bathroom, and since they only had one-gender bathrooms, the bathroom had to be evacuated for me. I would be lying if I said it felt easygoing being the only woman in the military barracks, not wondering when the last time had been that those guys had seen a woman. Thankfully, we did not spend much time there, probably about an hour or less. Another couple of vehicles arrived with our luggage, and we were packed up and ready to go.

We were surrounded by military personnel. I had never thought about going into the military. However, there were times that I felt like some of the experiences we, doctors, shared could be compared to stories that war-time comrades shared.

Chicago, USA 2014

I remember one cold morning in January 2014 when I had just completed a 24-hour shift and planned to nap at the hospital before I went home so I would not risk an accident. Then, I got paged the first time, the second time, and by the third time, I just gave up and got myself a cup of coffee. I called the Emergency Room.

"Hi, this is Dr. Akhras. I was paged."

"Hey! It's Joe." I smiled because Joe was one of my favorite pediatric emergency medicine doctors; he was brilliant, and when he called, it was usually because it was a complex case. So, I was intrigued by the case he was about to present. Knowing how to deal with routine cases is comforting, but I still love what I do after two decades of practice because of mentally challenging issues. They keep me reading and prevent me from becoming arrogant.

"I have this 15-year-old kid," Joe began, "with a week of feeling run down, fatigue, no real fevers at home but 102 here, stiff neck. So, I will tap him and start antibiotics and wanted you to consult."

"Sure," I said.

"He's going to CT first, and I have some labs pending; I am going to admit him to the intermediate care unit," Joe informed me.

"Okay," I replied. "How long before he gets up there?" I asked.

"I don't know. Maybe about an hour."

"Can I just come down and see him in the ER?"

He was surprised because the subspecialists there rarely ever did that. "Yeah, that would be great!"

"Okay, I'll be there in 10 minutes."

Usually, I am not particularly eager to go to the ER to see the patients there either. I don't know; maybe it brings back too many traumatic memories from residency when I would always see them in the ER and get my admission and orders done. There was no use getting woken up twice: once for the ER to tell you about the patient and another time when they finally made it up to the floor.

As I walked back to the ER, a technician wheeled the patient back from CT. I found Joe.

"Thanks for coming so quickly." He smiled.

"Believe me, it's no noble gesture on my end; I just completed a night shift and wanna get out of here and don't want to have to come back, Joe," I said.

He pulled up the CT and started scrolling. I stood behind him, looking over his shoulders. "What's this?" He asked when something abnormal popped up on the CT.

"I don't know, but I don't think it's me (meaning, "infectious")." He kept scrolling, and it only got worse.

"Yeah, I agree. I don't think it's you, either, but maybe, they are abscesses."

"Too big and too many for him to be walking around with. Anyway, I will stick around until radiology calls."

The radiologist called. *Brain mets.* I heard Joe saying, "Yeah, I am going to get an MRI," before he hung up. We exchanged a glance. One glance. One second. But in that glance, so much went unsaid, yet understood on both sides. We both knew what "brain mets" meant. The patient had cancer somewhere else that metastasized to his brain. That was the moment one family's lives changed forever. In that brief second, Joe and I shared a type of war-buddy camaraderie, including that dreaded conversation. In other words, the "bad news" conversation, which is *the worst, actually*. I looked over at him with raised eyebrows and a wrinkled forehead. In that one look, he knew I meant: "I am sorry you are about to go in there and do this now, but I am so glad that I am not you right now."

Yemen 2017

Such thoughts lead me back to the journey to Ma'rib in our military caravan. We drove through bumpy, desert terrain surrounded by mountains. And we moved fast. We had to keep up a certain speed to avoid heat-seeking missiles that could potentially target our vehicles. Again, I capitalized on my ability to compartmentalize. Instead of worrying about being surrounded by military officers carrying weapons, I took in the views of the vast, majestic desert, the sun reflecting off the golden pearls of sand.

We had broken up into two groups: John and I were in one car, and Zaher and Faiz were in the other. We generally kept this grouping throughout the whole trip. It served us well because the pediatricians and the internists stayed together. Also, this configuration kept an Arabic-speaking individual in each group.

The driver of our car and the leader of the military team driving us was a young Saudi officer who had trained at West Point Academy and was fluent in English, Commander Tameem. He had curly hair, dark eyes, and a small goatee. Of course, there was much small talk during the journey, but one of the tidbits that stuck with me was when he told us, "It's pretty safe here, but not that safe. Someone could sell you to ISIS for $100." I had never thought about myself as a commodity until then; I guess as an American physician in Yemen, that is how I could be perceived. Should I have been offended that we were worth only $100? Later, I heard about my actual net worth. Rumor had it that ISIS had a bounty out on Americans: $200,000 for a shot American and $1 million for a kidnapped one.

Armored vehicles and a caravan of military personnel were how we moved around during our week in Yemen. It was cumbersome but necessary.

At the halfway mark to Ma'rib, the caravan came to a stop. We were in the middle of nowhere, in the desert, with the sun beating down on us. They told us to get out and quickly into the following armored vehicles. This transition had to be quick. No lingering. No time to smell the fresh air. A different military team was picking us up. Our original unit did not have to drive to Ma'rib for six hours and back to where they were stationed for another six hours. It felt like a scene out of the movie *Syriana* (a 2005 political American thriller starring A-listers George Clooney and Matt Damon).

Another three hours went by until we finally reached our hotel in Ma'rib. It was a sepia-toned building curved in the back around a Mickey-Mouse-shaped pool. Our rooms were on the highest, 3rd floor, at the best hotel in the province. We were instructed to take the stairs to our rooms, and our bags would be brought up. I climbed up the stairs, pulling myself on the railings after a grueling day of travel. The clear globe lights cascaded from the ceiling. Finally, we convened in one of the rooms and asked to be left alone. We were all a little traumatized by the experience of driving as soldiers, guns, and trucks. I could tell none of us expected this. The first one to speak was Zaher. "This is worse than Aleppo," he said.

To give some perspective, he meant this experience was worse than when he and John had to hightail it out of Aleppo, Syria, as the bombs and sniper fire were raining down on them before Costello Road closed. Costello was the only highway in and out of Aleppo.

He then turned to me. "I am sorry I brought you here."

CHAPTER FIFTEEN

The Misogyny

We were staying in the best hotel in the city. In a city like Ma'rib, that meant very limited wi-fi with few chances to contact my family. The room had a boxed air-conditioning unit. The toilet seat in my bathroom was broken but since the toilet functioned, I did not complain. The only option in the shower was cold water. I capitalized on the temperature outside being above 90 degrees Fahrenheit to make myself hot enough to withstand a cold, three-minute shower. I was thankful for my ability to go with the flow.

The team's first order of business was to meet with the head of the only tertiary care center, Ma'rib General Hospital. He was a general surgeon, and we met him at the hotel restaurant after we had gotten some time to change into fresh clothes, clean up and rest. It had been a grueling 48 hours getting there, and early pregnancy fatigue was not helping. I was utterly exhausted then, and my face did not hide it. After the formal introductions, the general surgeon turned to me and said, "You look exhausted. You should rest since you are a woman. I can meet with the men."

Seriously? Pick your battles, Nour.

I made the quick decision to take him up on his suggestion. "Yes, you are right. I am exhausted, so I will take you up on that and excuse myself." I went up to my room to sleep.

I am not a stranger to misogyny. There is plenty of misogyny in medicine, whether among physicians who are supposed to be equal or in the physician-patient relationship when a physician is a man and the patient is a woman or the patient's guardian is a woman. I have been privileged enough to experience all three.

Ann Arbor, USA 2008

When I had my first baby, I had extensive complications requiring the attention of the on-call obstetrician for surgical repair. The on-call physician happened to be a man. I had extensive bleeding from birth to a hemoglobin of 7 (average is 12). Had I been in an underdeveloped country, I probably would have died in childbirth. No doubt, this physician saved my life that night.

Fast forward six weeks, and I was in excruciating pain and unable to get up and around. It was New Year's weekend, and most places were closed. I called the on-call physician, and I got the fellow. She told me this was probably normal and to keep taking ibuprofen. I had been taking ibuprofen around the clock for the last six weeks, but now the pain was so much worse. Amjad finally insisted that we go to the ER.

"Maybe I have an abscess," I said.

Several blood tests and CT scan later, everything turned out negative. I was discharged from the ER to go home. I knew I had high pain tolerance, but things were not adding up. I was still in a lot of pain, and the doctors told me nothing was there. I went home. The pain had not subsided, so Amjad insisted on taking me back to the ER.

"This isn't right," he said. "They can't just keep sending you home in this amount of pain."

We returned to the ER two more times before I was finally admitted. They discovered the abscess I had suspected and told them about earlier in the week. However, by then, it was already starting to drain spontaneously. I should have been livid that no one took me seriously. But I was in too much pain to care, too much emotional turmoil as a first-time mom. My baby could not get the nursing thing down properly since I had been in and out of the hospital for the past week. My OB/GYN scheduled an outpatient MRI for the following week.

I went to the appointment and changed into a gown. An IV was started, and the technician told me he would administer gadolinium (a contrast dye) to clarify the picture. He said, "It will feel warm, and that is normal." The gadolinium was infused, and it did feel warm. The MRI took an hour to complete. Once it was over, the tech returned to take my IV out and help me out of the machine.

Something was not right. I did not feel right. I was dizzy. My lips were chattering. I could not stand up. My doctor was already in the radiology suite because he was trying to look at the images. He came into the room I was in.

"What's going on?" He asked.

"I don't know. Something isn't right. I don't feel right," I replied.

He felt my forehead. No fever. I needed to sit down, and the tech brought me a wheelchair.

"You just need to relax." My doctor instructed.

"Maybe, I am septic [infection spread through my bloodstream causing abnormalities in my vital signs]."

"I think you are just anxious. You think you have sepsis because you are an ID fellow and everything seems infectious to you," he replied.

I may not have had sepsis, but I certainly was not anxious. I am one of the calmest people I know. But this was what my doctor told me, and I wondered whether or not I should consider the possibility. Could it have been my mind causing these symptoms? His fellow, a young woman, suggested getting a set of vitals on me. They wheeled me into another room and slapped a pulse ox on me and an automatic blood pressure cuff. My pulse was in the 150s (normal 70-90), my pulse ox was in the low 80s (normal is > 94), and my blood pressure was 180/110 (my average value is 90/60). Something was wrong with me, and I was not just anxious.

My doctor saw my vitals and freaked out. He told his fellow to wheel me down to the ER *stat*. I was having an anaphylactic reaction to the gadolinium.

In an article published in the *New York Times* in May 2018, Camile Noe Pagan highlights the studies that demonstrate the implicit bias against women as patients in medicine[7]:

"But research on disparities between how women and men are treated in medical settings is growing — and it is concerning for any woman seeking care. Research shows that both doctors and nurses prescribe less pain medication to women than men after surgery, even though women report more frequent and severe pain levels. And a University of Pennsylvania study found that women waited 16 minutes longer than men to receive pain medication when they visited an emergency room. Women are also more likely to be told their pain is 'psychosomatic' or influenced by emotional distress. And in a survey of more than 2,400 women with chronic pain, 83 percent said they felt they had experienced gender discrimination from their health care providers."

At the time, I was upset about how my physician dismissed me. In retrospect, however, that encounter was one of the most significant learning moments in my career as a physician. It taught me never to discount a patient's (or the patient's parent's) complaint or worry. There is an edict in pediatric medicine: always listen to a mother; she knows her child best. I have taken that mandate much more seriously since my experience was dismissed.

Ann Arbor, USA 2010

Misogyny is displayed against female patients. And it isn't that much different for female physicians. Many of us have faced sexism from the moment we entered medical school until far and beyond residency, fellowship, and practicing as a physician. When I graduated fellowship, there were not many openings for pediatric infectious diseases specialists in Michigan, so I worked as a pediatric hospitalist at a tertiary care center where a pediatric infectious diseases department existed. The head of the pediatric department was a strong woman. I had discussed with her that part of what drew me to this institution was the infectious diseases department. I was hoping I could do a few weeks during the year on the ID service. She was amenable and told me to speak to the head of the ID division.

We decided on an initial phone conversation after I sent him my CV. I was home when he called, and my one-year-old son was running around. Less than two minutes into the conversation, when he heard my son, he said, "The pediatric hospitalist schedule would be better for a mom of a young child such as yourself: I think you should stick to hospitalist medicine."

That was the end of the conversation.

In retrospect, I wish I had complained about him to the department head about how completely sexist that comment was, how he did not even give me a chance, and how I am sure he would have never said that to a man. But I didn't.

Chicago, USA 2015

Sometimes, the sexism is not so blatant, and the subtlety was perhaps why I did not complain; I did not notice it at the time. One day in February 2015, my two older children were off at school, and Amjad was away in Denver for a business trip. I was at home with my eleven-month-old son, Zaid. I noticed that he had these intermittent episodes of crunching his knees up, crying, and profuse sweating. They lasted for a couple of minutes and then resolved independently. I thought to myself: *he is too young to have intussusception* (a medical emergency during which the intestine telescope into each other, and if it lasts for too long, there could be a compromise to the blood supply of the bowels and part of the bowel could die, which could lead to massive infection in the child and ultimately, death). Zaid had these episodes a couple of more times.

I called Amjad. "I think Zaid is sick," I said to him after I greeted him over the phone.

"What's wrong with him?" He asked.

"I think he might have intussusception," I replied.

"What's that?" He inquired.

"It's a medical condition in which the intestines telescope into each other. If not treated early enough, his intestines could die, and he would need emergency surgery."

"Why do you think he has that?"

I explained what I had noticed. He told me to call our pediatrician, Dr. Bond. Dr. Bond was a general pediatrician who was very friendly and everything. However, he and I knew I was more sub-specialized than he was, and he always deferred to me. Back then, I became frustrated with my husband whenever he recommended calling another physician because I thought he did not think I was smart enough. But it turned out, he only suggested calling another physician because he, himself, felt helpless in giving a second opinion. All he could think of was recommending that I bounce the ideas off someone else who was medically trained.

I called Dr. Bond and sure enough, he recommended I take Zaid for an ultrasound.

I strapped him in his car seat because it was his nap time, and I got myself ready and he did it again. I packed an overnight bag for him and me because I became more confident that we would spend the night in the hospital. The hospital where I worked was 45 minutes away. Despite the ability to go to a closer option, I thought my colleagues at work would be more likely to do what I requested, instead of another set of healthcare workers who did not know me from Sally.

I was triaged, and thankfully, it was slow in the ER. I was taken in right away, and the ER physician who was going to assess my son was a colleague of mine who called me frequently for consultations regarding complicated pediatric infectious diseases cases.

"What seems to be the problem, Nour?" Tim asked me as Zaid smiled at him and the two medical students Tim was teaching.

"I think Zaid has intussusception."

"Is he having blood in his stool?" Tim asked. That is one of the signs, but probably a later sign.

"No."

"Then?" He looked puzzled.

I described the episodes to Tim. He told me to undress my baby so that he could examine him. The whole time, Zaid smiled and interacted playfully with his big, bright brown eyes and long eyelashes.

Tim was teaching as he examined Zaid playfully. He explained intussusception to the students and quizzed them on medical management.

After he was done, he turned to the students and said, "This is what a baby who does not have intussusception looks like."

He just dismissed me. My colleague, who always calls me for an opinion on managing complicated patients, just dismissed me. *Unbelievable.*

"Just humor me, Tim, and get the ultrasound," I pleaded.

"Okay. I will order it."

Ten minutes later, we were being wheeled to the radiology suite, where a tech put jelly on my baby's belly and moved the probe in multiple directions, snapping pictures as she went. I tried to see if I could make out anything, but I was not a trained radiologist, and I was trying to keep him calm and still so she could get the most accurate images.

"Wait here, and I will be right back," she said.

"Is there something wrong?" I asked.

"No. I have to show the images to the radiologist and see if he wants any other views before I can wheel you guys back to the ER."

"Does he have intussusception?" I asked. I knew she was not supposed to tell me even if she saw it, but I could not help myself; it was my baby.

"We will have to wait for the radiologist to read the images." She smiled politely.

Five minutes later, which seemed like fifty years, she returned. "He doesn't need any more images. We are good to go."

As she wheeled us back to the ER, I heard the overhead paging system: 'Dr. Conrad, please call 3462 STAT. Dr. Conrad 3462 STAT."

Dr. Conrad was the pediatric surgeon on call for the week, and 3642 was the ER phone number. I knew that was for us.

Tim walked inside with a sheepish grin as soon as we were back in our little ER room. "Zaid has intussusception."

Tears trickled down my face. I had said these words to many families before. I did not think twice about it because I knew the next step was to call radiology to try to reduce it with a barium enema. Most of the time, that worked; it was usually not a big deal, and the family would be discharged the next day. However, when it was my baby, and I knew what the potential complications looked like and how things could go sour, it was a different ball game.

Thankfully, Zaid's intussusception was reduced in the radiology suite. They monitored him overnight. There was no recurrence, and we were sent home the next day without further complications.

That night at the hospital, after Zaid fell asleep in the crib, I could not help but think to myself: *why was it so easy for Tim to dismiss me?* Yes, my baby looked good, but would he ever have had the audacity to tell his medical students that the baby did not have the diagnosis I suspected if I were his male colleague bringing in my child before he even did the study?

I was too exhausted to imagine the possibility.

How many -isms and -phobias *can* one or *does* one need to battle?

CHAPTER SIXTEEN

The Terror

Yemen 2017

The next day in Yemen, we met at the hotel lobby. When one of my teammates asked me how I was doing, I revealed that I had traveler's diarrhea. John said he had ciprofloxacin (an antibiotic) if I wanted it. *Is that safe during pregnancy?* We looked it up. It was category C. That means adverse effects have been seen in the fetus in animal studies, but not enough data exists in human studies. I decided to push fluids aggressively and take the antibiotic because dehydration can also cause adverse effects. We had breakfast which, for me, consisted of tea and yogurt. Then, we boarded our cumbersome caravan to the tertiary care facility, Ma'rib General Hospital.

Hundreds of patients and families showed up, hearing of the team of American physicians who had come to Ma'rib. Dr. Mohamed, the head of the hospital, welcomed us. The plan was to give us a tour of the hospital before we got down to work. We were the first Western physicians to have visited the province in more than ten years.

Everything was immaculate. A lot of effort was put into preparing for our visit. Part of the preparation included deeply cleaning the hospital. As soon as we walked in, I was overwhelmed by the smell of the cleaning chemicals. It smelled like Clorox, Comet, Lysol, Pinesol, and every other cleaning product known to humanity. The scent was exacerbating my morning sickness.

They showed us the outpatient parts of the hospital first. We saw where they made and fit prosthetic limbs, the imaging center, and the laboratory. Then they took us up to the wards. I was doing what I could to keep up and not faint or throw up. It became blatantly apparent that their equipment was outdated and that the pharmacy and blood bank were inadequately stocked, particularly for a region plagued by war.

We finally got upstairs to the wards; the hospital rooms had 8-10 beds per room. No curtains between anybody. All the patients were middle-aged men until we got to the one and only child in the hospital.

This was the tertiary care hospital for the whole province. There used to be a pediatric ward, but they had to shut it down to make room for the adults injured from the bombings who had been coming in from neighboring provinces.

Dr. Mohammed motioned for me to examine the child. His name was Naji. He was 12, but he looked like he was eight years old. Malnutrition had stunted his growth. Naji had stepped on a land mine, and shrapnel tore through his chest. He went to the OR for shrapnel removal. A couple of days after that, he developed a GI bleed. Patients can develop bleeding ulcers in their stomachs from stress and being kept without feeding. In the US, we usually give preventative medication to these patients, GI prophylaxis. The Yemeni physicians were not aware of that data.

Naji looked scared. He was in respiratory distress, his chest moving up and down quickly. I listened to his racing heart, trying to compensate for the lack of oxygen. As I stood over him, watching him breathe, my nausea worsened.

The hospital only had one ventilator. Naji probably would end up needing it, but a more dire patient was using it.

Unfortunately, Naji never made it out of the hospital alive.

In Arabic, *Naji* means "the one who survived."

As we moved on in the tour, I finally said, "I have to sit down."

As the hospital administrators continued showing my colleagues another part of the hospital, I grabbed a chair and took a seat.

Then, I heard someone comment, "She can't handle seeing these injured patients."

Of course not, because I am a woman, the bleeding and amputated limbs were so much for me that I could faint.

Luckily, one of my colleagues did not let it go. "She does this thing daily. This is her job. She can handle it."

Thank you. Someone gets it.

Ma'rib is 75 miles east of Sana'a, the capital of Yemen. Before the conflict, the population was about 20,000 people. By the time we arrived, the population had tripled. And still, they had only one tertiary care hospital with one ventilator. *Insane!* Before the conflict, Yemen's medical infrastructure was deplorable, and the war only exacerbated this.

After the hospital tour, we split into two groups. The pediatricians, John and I, were taken to one area, and the internists, Zaher and Faiz, were taken to another.

I started seeing patients. Some common cases were upper respiratory tract infections, ear infections, vomiting, and diarrhea. I saw a lot of parasitic diseases and so many children who were physically smaller than their stated age—chronic malnutrition. I gave the malnourished children vitamins. That is all I could offer; I knew that was not a cure. They needed the borders and the airports to be opened so humanitarian aid could enter efficiently and freely. I did not have control over that, but I remained hopeful that our trip highlighted the humanitarian crisis in Yemen. In that light, I was so happy to share the details of my journey on Chicago Public Radio's Worldview, after which I returned.

I drank a lot of soda in Yemen. That was not part of my everyday diet, although I must admit, I lived on Coke when I was in college. I consumed many forms of caffeine. As a junior, I had to take a mandatory geology class even though I had taken many science classes since I was a science major. In any case, I took this class that the students had nicknamed "rocks for jocks." It was the first thing in the morning on my schedule. Some days, I did not have time for a proper breakfast, having stayed up the night before studying until 2 AM, like I did every night. I grabbed a Coke and a Snickers bar (*I know, very nutritious*) and sat in the front row, still falling asleep every time. (*Sorry, Professor. I hope you did not take it personally*). In Yemen, however, I expected that the chemicals and processing used to make the soda would have killed all the bacteria known to humanity and would not further contribute to my GI symptoms.

I also ate many bananas. I felt terrible because everywhere we went, a feast was offered to us. The elaborate banquets consisted of meals like *haneeth* (a slow-roasted lamb slathered in spices served over a bed of rice) and *sayadieh* (fish bathed in caramelized onions submerged in tomato paste and sprinkled with cumin, turmeric, and cinnamon). When I entered the rooms where these elaborate meals were served, wafts of ginger, cardamom, mint, and cilantro filled the air. I craved bananas. My body was probably compensating for the loss of potassium.

One day, the hotel chef, Adnan, came out of the kitchen in his bright white toque and apron into the hotel's banquet room. I was sitting on one of the red chairs with a golden frame with an empty plate in front of me while my colleagues were heartily digging in for lunch.

"How are you, Doctor Nour?" Adnan asked, his warm personality beaming through his smile. He wiped his hands on his apron.

"I am good. How about yourself?"

"I am very well. I see you don't have anything on your plate. Is something wrong?"

"I am just feeling a little unwell from the traveling," I replied. I did not want to hurt his feelings, but I was not planning to share the news of my pregnancy unnecessarily.

"What can I get you?"

"Do you have a boiled potato?" I just wanted something bland. That was not something Adnan was expecting or was prepared to make. He left and came back after fifteen minutes with my request.

"We didn't have one in the back, so I went home and asked my wife to make it for you."

I was so touched by the hospitality and generosity the Yemeni people displayed amid all their hardships.

After spending the first day at the hospital, we returned to our hotel for a late lunch and rest. The group decided we would do some sightseeing in the afternoon. I told them I might pass because I was not feeling so well. I went to my hotel room and passed out. It was 90 degrees Fahrenheit outside, and the air conditioner was a box unit. The options were: full blast or bake in your room. I mostly had the air conditioner on. It was loud and obnoxious and made the room cold, so I wore a sweatshirt and dove deep under the blankets. My team knocked on my door when it was time to leave, but I was dead to the world and did not hear anything. They assumed I was asleep and let me be.

Around 3 in the afternoon, the phone in my hotel room rang.

"Hello?"

A man's voice in Arabic asked, "Is Hamza there?"

"No, you've got the wrong room."

"Sorry." *Click.*

I tried to go back to sleep, but the phone call spooked me a little. Twenty minutes later, there was a knock on my door. *Thank God they are back.* I went to open the door, and two men in military fatigue with their weapons strapped on were standing at my door.

"Sorry, wrong room." One of them said as soon as he saw me. I closed the door.

Now I was completely freaking out—sheer terror. I was at the hotel, all alone, while my team had gone sight-seeing with the military caravan. Perhaps a few soldiers were left behind because I was still there, although I was not sure. Everyone at the hotel knew that we were there. Everybody in the Province knew because no one could miss our military escort. I was there alone, a sitting duck!

"Anyone could sell you to ISIS for $100," I remembered Commander Tameem's statement.

The mind has a fantastic way of proposing multiple scenarios at lightning speed when a person feels threatened.

My mind immediately thought of Peter Kassig and Muath al-Kassasbeh. *How would I be able to get out of a kidnapping situation?* I was Muslim, but that was not enough to save Peter and Muath. *What if I told them I was taught to read Qur'an by some of the most highly qualified teachers of the Qur'an in the world in Damascus? What if I recited the verses in the Qur'an that clarify that whoever takes the life of an innocent soul, it is as if he has killed all of humanity, and whoever saves the life of an innocent soul, it is as if he has saved all of humanity.* I was sure that would not work on the senior leadership of such a hateful and skewed organization, but maybe, someone very junior? *I mean, who else would they put to guard a woman besides a guy in a junior position of ISIS? Perhaps if I told them I was pregnant? Or that I was a mom of three children at home waiting for me, the youngest of whom was only three years old? Would that work?*

I wondered if they would have mercy on me because I was a woman. Nadia Murad came to mind. Nadia was a 21-year-old Yazidi woman when ISIS took over her village, slaughtered over 300 men, and took the young women as "spoils of war." She was gang-raped multiple times and managed to escape when one of her captors forgetfully left the door unlocked. Since then, she has been represented by human rights lawyer Amal Clooney. After remembering what I had read about Murad's case, I decided that ISIS extremists did not know the meaning of mercy.

I was sure Amjad would try to raise the money to ransom me should I become imprisoned. I thought about James Foley and the US policy of never negotiating with terrorists. James Foley was a freelance journalist covering the war in Syria when he was kidnapped in November 2012. ISIS eventually beheaded him in August 2014. His family harshly criticized the US government's lack of help even though the government sent a special ops team to rescue Foley and fellow kidnapped American freelance journalist Steven Sotloff. That campaign failed, and Sotloff was also murdered soon after Foley. These were white American men, born and raised, and the government could not negotiate for their freedom. My chances were much lower, I thought.

After an hour of this marathon that ran through my mind, another knock came on my door. At that point, I was contemplating whether or not I should open the door. When I heard "It's me, John" from the hallway, my reaction was, *THANK GOD!*

"We drove around the whole city to find you some bananas!" He said.

He handed them to me. The bananas in Yemen were much smaller than the ones I was used to in the states. No GMO (genetically modified organism).

"Thanks. I am so glad you guys are back. I was starting to worry."

He told me about their tourist adventures. They went to see the sanctuary of the Queen of Sheba. This figure is mentioned in all three monotheistic traditions of Islam, Christianity, and Judaism as a powerful woman who brings gifts to King Solomon. Her visit was heralded by the hoopoe, who told Solomon of a kingdom of sun worshippers. How ironic that just outside this city filled with people who believe me to be of an inferior gender, was a sanctuary of a queen who lived thousands of years ago and was thought to be quite adept at ruling an entire kingdom. I would have liked to have visited the sanctuary. But alas, the baby I was carrying had different plans for us.

John also told me that the group went to a facility that rehabilitated child soldiers, another place I would have liked to have visited.

The facility focused on the physical and psycho-social rehabilitation of the boys who were forced into active combatant roles in the conflict in Yemen. The facility was run by the WHO (World Health Organization), and it was in better condition than the only tertiary care hospital we had visited earlier.

I never told my team about how scared I was when they were gone. But I vowed to not separate from them again while we remained in Yemen. I also never shared this part of the mission with most of my close family and friends. That night, I made a heartfelt prayer to God for keeping me safe once again, renewed my resolve to use the resources available to me to help others.

CHAPTER SEVENTEEN

The Discovery

The next day, we went back to the same hospital. A public announcement had been made that a team of American physicians was seeing patients at the hospital. Patients traveled far distances to come to see us. We had brought our supplies, including over 200 pounds of medications like antibiotics, analgesics, inhalers, nebulizers, blood pressure medications, steroids, and IV fluids.

The line of patients was long, and I was feeling somewhat better. I asked for a chair to sit on, which isn't my standard practice when I tend to patients, but I didn't want my dizziness to hinder me in any way. "He doesn't walk. He does not talk. She does not have complete control of her limbs. She can't swallow well." Patient after patient. I asked for the history, and it was quite similar. The defects had been there from the very beginning. Some families had CT scans to show me, and when I said that it appeared that their child had cerebral palsy, no one seemed surprised.

As the day went on, it became more apparent that these parents already knew that their child had cerebral palsy. However, they were hoping that the American pediatrician had a cure. The overall prevalence of cerebral palsy in the United States is two cases per 1000 live births. The risk is higher in preterm infants and exceptionally high for babies without oxygen in the perinatal period. I knew that we probably had a selection bias, so we were seeing more cases than the average pediatrician would see in Yemen because people thought we would have some magical cure. However, still, the numbers seemed too high.

I started asking, "Where was your baby born?" The parents named the city or town.

"No, where was the mother when the baby was delivered? Was she at home or at a hospital?"

Most women delivered at home, it turned out. After meeting with the local health authorities, we learned that there were roughly 30,000 live births in Ma'rib province annually. Out of those, 9,000 women had some prenatal care. A healthcare worker attended only 3000 births, and 99% of those healthcare workers were midwives.

"Are the midwives trained in attending to the neonates?" I asked the health minister of Ma'rib.

"No, they just tend to the mother."

"Who tends to the baby?" I thought I did not understand what he was saying.

"No one."

WHAT?!

I could not believe what I had just heard. This was a city, not a rural area; there were doctors and a hospital. It was 2017! And no one tended to the baby? Was the baby just delivered and put down somewhere as the midwife delivered the placenta and tended to the mother's health?

Having attended hundreds of deliveries as a pediatrician, I could not wrap my head around that. No one assessed if the baby was crying, breathing well, or anything?

Pediatricians who work in American hospitals with nurseries eat, sleep and drink Apgar scores. The Apgar score was developed in the 1950s by an anesthesiologist, Virginia Apgar. It is a quick method to summarize the newborn's health based on the baby's appearance, pulse, grimace, activity, and respiration. For each category, a baby gets a score from 0-2, and the scores are added up at 1 minute and 5 minutes of life. A low score at 10 minutes of life may indicate long-term neurologic damage—low scores at 1 minute of life prompt immediate intervention by healthcare workers.

No one graduates medical school in the United States without knowing what an Apgar score is. However, it seemed they had not even heard of it in Yemen.

The next day, I was supposed to lecture on infection control and prevention in the hospital. It was widely attended by doctors, nurses, respiratory therapists, and management. I focused on hand hygiene as the number one, two, and three most effective ways to prevent the spread of disease in and outside of the hospital. I talked about contact, droplet, and airborne precautions and when and where these were supposed to be implemented. Unsurprisingly, most attendants were men.

In the middle of my lecture, I decided to switch gears and talk about neonatal resuscitation. I may save a life by teaching about how to prevent the spread of infection from patient to patient. But I also thought preventing neurologic devastation in children was a high priority. I found it extremely unfair that a baby born in Yemen could not benefit from the most up-to-date medical information. During this critical period in an infant's life, the intervention to prevent oxygen loss is so simple. This whole situation profoundly disturbed me.

I did not know or care who was attending. I even wanted the cleaning team (who was also primarily male) to hear what I had to say, and I let the audience know to invite them. I started by saying that at some point in your life, you, your spouse, or someone in your family will have a baby, and I want you to be prepared to give the baby the best chance possible. The child and family are not the only ones who suffer when a child has a disability. The whole of society is affected.

I felt very strongly about addressing this topic when I could work with anyone. I brought it up at our multiple meetings, including with the advisor to the Prime Minister of Yemen, the Governor of Ma'rib Province, and the province's health director. These meetings usually consisted of many men and myself. At first, it seemed odd, and I felt uncomfortable being the only woman in all the gatherings and meetings. However, just as I had gotten used to everyone around us carrying some weapon, I became accustomed to being the only woman in these meetings. Everyone was accommodating to me, hospitable, and quite warm. It was easy to get comfortable.

Soon after my return from Yemen, MedGlobal initiated the Helping Babies Breathe training programs in Yemen and Bangladesh. This internationally-recognized program reduces infant mortality by training people in administering life-saving measures during the "Golden Minute" (the first minute after birth). I am proud to have been on the Board of an organization teaching people how to fish, not just giving them fish.

CHAPTER EIGHTEEN

The Return

Our original plan was to stay for a few more days in Ma'rib. Still, on that Thursday evening, we were watching the CNN equivalent in Yemen when we heard that the Houthis had shot down a Coalition Forces fighter jet and that a Saudi fighter pilot had been killed.

"Uh-oh. Things are about to escalate," Zaher said.

All week, we had been trying to brainstorm how we would get out of Yemen without going through that 6-hour miserable drive in the desert terrain. One of the few options was to drive to the Yemeni-Saudi border, which was only a two-hour drive, and then take a military helicopter to the closest Saudi airport. Our team had been trying to work on this all week, but it was not coming to fruition. After much deliberation and all other options being denied, we succumbed to the idea that we would have to make the same grueling six-hour trip back.

"There is a Yemenia Airways flight going out to Cairo tomorrow morning from Sey'oun," Mahmood, our local NGO collaborator, told us. It was now near midnight. We were not completely packed yet, and the flight was going to leave at 7 AM.

"We won't make it in time," John said.

"Oh, sure you will. That flight never leaves on time. You will make it." Mahmood said.

"Okay. Let's go, then. Everybody pack up and be back with your luggage in 15 minutes," Zaher instructed.

Everyone had brought a carry-on, so it was not that hard. The Governor of Ma'rib had gifted every team member with some Yemeni memorabilia. He gave me a Yemeni doll for my children, a stuffed toy camel, a small iconic Yemeni mud high-rise, and a big tub of much coveted Yemeni honey. We waited outside for our military convoy to be rounded up. Some of the hotel employees waited outside with us. It was a cool night. The bright moon peeked through the grand palm trees that towered over us. As we made small talk, waiting, I heard the familiar sweet sound of a strumming Spanish guitar. I turned around, and a young man who worked at the hotel was watching something on his phone with the song *Despacito* in the background.

Wow. Despacito has made it to Yemen, but not Apgars!

The military caravan was assembled, and we headed for our armored vehicles. By then, most of the group knew I was pregnant. The driver motioned me to sit next to him in the front. This was almost unheard of in this ultra-conservative province for a woman to sit up front next to a man she was not related to. Nevertheless, I welcomed the compassion.

I sat next to the driver and tried to recline the seat back a little. I knew what to expect and hoped I could fall asleep because it would be a long night. The driver handed me his assault rifle. It is funny what human beings can normalize. If you had told me before I left Chicago that I would get used to people walking around armed, I would have thought you were crazy. However, here it was, 1 AM local time, and we were trying to get out of Yemen before the war escalated. I found it utterly normal that I was holding our driver's gun.

The trip back was not as bad because we knew what to expect, and the blazing sun was not beating down on us because it was nighttime. But it was still stressful.

Many people in Yemen chew *qat*. It is a leafy plant native to the Arabian Peninsula that was a stimulant. They chew it and then store it in one of their cheeks so they look like a half-chipmunk. It is classified as a drug of abuse by the World Health Organization. In the US, it is considered a controlled substance.

Great. All we need is for our driver to be high as a kite as we hightail it out of this country.

But by then, I was smart enough to know that a high driver was the least of my worries. I welcomed the thundering of the armored vehicles as our caravan roared ahead and lulled me to sleep. Seven-and-a-half hours and many checkpoints later, we had finally arrived at the small Sey'oun airport that we had flown into earlier that week. We looked to the lonely runway, but no plane was in sight. One of our security team members ran in to check us in.

"It left on time today," he relayed.

Plan B. We had to improvise. We went in to purchase our tickets for the next day's flight and then proceeded to find a hotel in Sey'oun.

"I know of a good hotel," one of the Yemeni NGO members said. He led the way.

We arrived and got down, as did all the soldiers traveling with us.

Mahmood greeted the receptionist and said, "We need six rooms." Four for the physicians, one for Mahmood, and one for the two Yemeni volunteers who came with us to help us make it out of the country.

The man at the reception desk looked at us, looked at the soldiers, then turned to his computer and back to us.

"We are booked solid for the night. I don't have any rooms for you."

Who is here visiting Yemen in the middle of the war? European tourists?

"No problem. Thanks for checking," Zaher replied.

Who can blame the hotel receptionist? Sey'oun had stayed relatively conflict-free up to this time. This man was not about to let some suspicious-looking people flagged by military personnel stay in his hotel and start trouble.

We drove out to another hotel. This time, we told the soldiers not to come in with us, and what do you know, we were granted six rooms right away!

It was midday, and we had been traveling all night. We got a quick bite to eat and decided to rest. We agreed to reconvene at 6 PM for dinner and maybe some sightseeing.

I got up to my room, and the air conditioner was blasting. I had a wi-fi signal. *Woohoo!* I turned on the water for the shower, and it was hot water. I felt like I had died and gone to heaven. I could take a real shower here. After cleaning up, I crawled into bed to nap and got back up after three hours to meet downstairs at the agreed-upon time.

Our Yemeni partners who traveled with us from Ma'rib decided to show us around Sey'oun. We saw some of the distinctive architecture of Sey'oun, which consisted of mud brick high-rises. We also toured the most prominent landmark in Sey'oun, the Palace. Although the sights were fascinating, all I kept thinking about was finally getting home. We got to the hotel late at night. We were still unsure that the flight would leave the next day even though we had purchased our tickets. In the lobby, we overheard a man talking on his cell phone. It turned out that he was the Yemenia Airways pilot who would be flying our plane out the next day if things were calm.

"How's it looking?" Zaher asked him.

"I don't know yet. The Coalition forces don't give the green light until after 11 PM."

"But what are the chances?" Zaher asked again.

"I think leaving looks good, but where we go is a different question. We may get the green light for Cairo or Amman."

What? Cairo or Amman? What is this? A bus? You fly us up and head to a different city at some point in mid-air? I translated for John and Faiz. By the end of our trip, we had heard it all, so no one was flustered. We were going to go with the flow. Even if we made it to Amman, we could book flights to Chicago. *Get us out of here before the war escalates, and all the airports close!*

Within the last 48 hours of our trip to Yemen, news started to trickle in of how the Myanmar military was conducting operations that included burning villages. Human rights violations and atrocities triggered a mass exodus of Rohingya refugees into Bangladesh. Zaher, the co-founder and president of the new medical NGO that we were all a part of, MedGlobal, was getting images texted to his phone. He was sharing the news with all of us.

"Look at these pictures. This is awful." He showed them to John, who turned away as soon as he saw them. Zaher directed the phone to me.

"No, thanks. I don't need to see graphic images. I believe you."

"We should plan to go there next. Bangladesh should be our target for the next medical mission," Zaher said.

Being in Sey'oun and finally having wi-fi. I had been texting Amjad to update him on how we had eventually left Ma'rib and were trying to fly out of Sey'oun the next day. I told him we were unsure what the destination city would be or if the flight was even going to take off.

"I don't care where that plane is going. You guys get on it!" He was getting worried.

"Have you been seeing the news about Myanmar?" I tried to change the subject.

"Yes."

"That's gonna be the destination of the next MedGlobal mission," I informed him.

"Okay."

"I am thinking about going."

Long pause.

"Okay."

"Are you crazy?! I am just kidding. There is no way I am going anywhere after this, for a long time after this baby is born!"

"I never know with you :)," he texted back.

The next day, we met early in the morning and headed to the airport. Everything looked like it was going as planned. We saw the pilot in the airport, and he gave us a thumbs up. We were heading to Cairo just as planned.

I had never been so relieved to board an airplane in my life. The plane took off, and all seemed well. Mid-air, we saw the pilot heading in our direction. He told us of the many times he had to fly over the last couple of years under extreme and dangerous circumstances. Once, the flight was over-filled with people, particularly injured people. There were people even sitting in the aisle. There was blood everywhere. The flight was already boarded, and the airplane door was closed when Coalition forces commanded him that he could not take off because it would be too dangerous. The runway lights were turned off. He decided to leave anyway. He had a plane full of injured people trying to get out to seek safety and medical attention elsewhere, and he would not disappoint them.

He told us, "I wanted you to know that I was going to do my best to get your team out of Yemen. I appreciate everything you guys have done for the Yemeni people by risking your lives and coming here. There was even a malfunction in the plane, but I said, 'let's go anyway' because I wanted to get your team out!"

Were we supposed to feel better about that? I thought to myself. He was flying a malfunctioning plane! Perhaps, it would have been better if he left that tiny tidbit to himself or told us after the fact. Regardless, I admired him for risking his life daily to save others.

Just as I have borne witness to the suffering of so many refugees I met in Turkey and Greece, I have also borne witness to the suffering of the Yemeni people. I feel that I have a responsibility to share what I saw. Two years later, on March 8, 2019, on International Women's Day, I accepted an award that I don't think I deserved: the "MedGlobal's Hero Award" for my work in Yemen. I accepted it so I could shed light on the crisis in Yemen. In my acceptance speech, I spoke of over 20 million people in Yemen, requiring humanitarian assistance, on the brink of famine. Some children were so malnourished that they did not even have the energy to cry. I asked the nearly 300 people celebrating the first annual MedGlobal Benefit dinner to commit with me to do something for these people. And now, I am also asking you, the reader, to join me in this commitment to dig deep, to push yourself to attain a transcendent mercy that will serve you well throughout your lifetime.

CHAPTER NINETEEN

The Little Secret

It seems every day, over the last few years, I have felt more urgently motivated to try to do something about the political climate of hate heralded by the election of Donald Trump. I went to sleep one Thursday night in March 2019 after reading the news that a white supremacist opened fire in a mosque filled with Friday prayer worshipers in Christchurch, New Zealand. More than 50 people were killed. He live-streamed his gruesome attack on social media. I did not watch the video, and I did not read his manifesto. The most poignant thing I saw on social media and what I did re-post was that the first person who was shot was the person who welcomed the shooter into the mosque, saying, "Hello, Brother." Like the Quebec Mosque shooter, the Christchurch shooter cited Donald Trump's actions as motivating factors. That was hard to stomach. The president of my country was a source of motivation for people to kill members of my faith.

We are not a TV-watching household. That was a conscious decision Amjad and I made when we got married and have been able to hold on to throughout our children's childhood. I also try not to listen to the news while my children are in the car. So as far as I knew, my kids had not heard about the shooting.

The day after the Christchurch shooting, when I picked up my children from school, my eldest son at the time, Hamza, ten years old, asked, "Mama, did someone shoot a bunch of Muslims at a mosque in New Zealand?"

Man! How did he hear that? I kept composed.

"Yes. That is true. Where did you hear that?" I asked him.

"My teacher told us," my son replied.

"Oh. Well, people shoot people all the time."

Wow, Nour. That was an absolute gem! I see a parent-of-the-century award in your future.

I did not want him to know that Muslims were singled out. He was too young to take that in, I thought. However, I was not sure telling him people get shot all the time was reassuring, either.

"Why? Why do people shoot people all the time?" He inquired.

So much of parenting is thinking on one's feet. We don't get it right a lot of the time.

"Because their mommas didn't teach them to love everybody," I managed.

I gave him an affectionate hug and kiss and rubbed his head. I made a mental note to re-address this conversation later that day or the next when better prepared.

I felt terrible blaming the moms. I was a mom. A mom could not take responsibility for everything their adult children chose to do. Nevertheless, I also cannot believe that so much of this hatred does not start in childhood and at home. Studies have consistently shown that mass shooters have a history of violent behavior, especially toward women. That starts at home, right? Did they witness their moms being victims of domestic violence? Were they, themselves, victims of domestic violence? Did no one protect them from violence? It is common knowledge that violence is a vicious cycle.

I do not doubt that hatred and the ability to commit vicious acts against another person only occur after the dehumanization process. Steven Dale, the American veteran of the Iraqi war, who was tried and convicted of raping and murdering 14-year-old Abeer Qassim al-Janabi and murdering her parents and little sister, told the *Daily Mail* in an interview that he did not think of them (Iraqis) as human.[8]

Over the past 20 years, I believe there has been a deliberate and systematic dehumanization of Muslims in the United States and elsewhere. How else could the Chapel Hill murders be explained? On

February 10, 2015, 48-year-old Craig Hicks walked into the apartment of newlyweds Deah Barakat, aged 23, and Yusor Abu Salha, aged 21, and shot them point blank in the head. Also murdered by the same perpetrator on that day, in that apartment, was Yusor's 19-year-old sister, Razan Abu Salha. Deah was a second-year dentistry student at the University of North Carolina, Chapel Hill. His wife, Yusor, graduated from North Carolina State University with a degree in biology and planned to enroll at UNC-Chapel Hill's dentistry school in the fall. Razan was a student of architecture and environmental design. All three were model students involved in charity and volunteer work in their spare time. The crime was initially deemed to have happened over a disputed parking spot. Still, the victims' families insisted that this was a hate crime because no one's car was parked in the disputed parking spot on the day of the murder. Tensions between Barakat and Hicks rose after his wife, Yusor, who wore a hijab, moved in.

I attended a medical conference in Arizona with Amjad and our two children, aged 6 and 4, at the time of the Chapel Hill murders. We were staying at an Airbnb in unfamiliar territory, and I had planned to go to Target to get some supplies for the week. It was late at night when news of the crime hit, and for the first time in my lifetime, I was too scared to go out in public wearing my hijab. My husband offered to go instead, but I knew I would not allow that to become my new norm. I did not let it after 9/11, and I was not about to, then, either.

Indeed, that was not the first or last hate crime against Muslims, but what made the Chapel Hill shootings so different was that they were model students and model citizens.

Just like the fact that Peter Kassig and Muath al-Kassasbeh supposedly shared the same religion as the ISIS members who murdered them, the fact that Deah, Yusor, and Razan were all-American kids who shared the same culture as Craig Hicks did not matter.

I say that Peter Kassig and Muath al-Kassasbeh supposedly shared the same religion as the ISIS members because I do not believe that ISIS represents Islam. Although I have never met Peter or Muath, I imagine they probably shared my tenets of faith rather than those of ISIS. The Islamophobic machine would have you believe Islam is inherently violent. In an opinion piece written by Simon Clark, a senior fellow at the Center for American Progress, he said: "There exists a plethora of organizations dedicated to spreading hate-filled, racist, Islamophobic and white nationalist messages under the guise of politics.[9]"

In 2016, the Council on American-Islamic Relations and the University of California at Berkley listed 74 groups that had invested $206 million into Islamophobic projects from 2008-2013. These include ACT for America's "Radicalization Map Locator," a database of nearly every Muslim student association and mosque in the US with no known links to violence.[10]"

What an insane use of 206 million dollars! How many poor people could that money feed? How much medical care could that provide? How many kids' educational programs could that secure? When people then turn around and demand from American Muslims what we are doing to combat "terrorism," the answer isn't spending 206 million dollars trying to spew lies and hatred about another religious or ethnic community.

You are not crazy if you think Muslims are more violent than others. You are a victim of this media culture. According to a study by the University of Alabama, terrorist attacks committed by Muslim extremists received 357% more news coverage in the United States than terror attacks committed by people of other religions.[11] In July 2018, the *Guardian* published this information:[12]

"The findings, which are illustrated below, were based on all terrorist attacks in the US between 2006 and 2015 according to the Global Terrorism Database. The disparity in media coverage is particularly out of sync with the reality given that white and right-wing terrorists carried out nearly twice as many terrorist attacks as Muslim extremists between 2008 and 2016."

We, as Americans, should ask ourselves why that is and what results from this overwhelming bias. I experienced the results first-hand when someone who had never met me before yelled out, "Go back to your country, terrorist," while I was crossing the street in hijab, the most visible symbol of Islam. I have many comebacks in my head for these brief comments, some of which are entirely inappropriate, none of which I have ever used.

In the decade after 9/11, people frequently asked Muslims to combat terrorists within our midst. They asked and expected us to apologize for every Muslim terrorist act committed. As a religious group, we found ourselves defending our religion and apologizing for the act committed in the name of our faith. We were grieving because Muslims were often also killed in these heinous crimes, and then, afraid for our lives or the lives of our children and loved ones from acts of retaliation. What are the mental health effects produced in this kind of environment? What kind of mental health effects will subsequent Islamophobic or xenophobic attacks, create?

In April 2018, the House Judiciary Committee held a hearing on the rise of white nationalism. Dr. Abu-Salha, a psychiatrist and father of the two university students executed in Chapel Hill, testified to likely being the only physician who had ever read the autopsy reports of his own two children. He testified how the details were seared into his mind. However, despite the subject of the hearing and the fact that this man's two young daughters were victims of a hate crime, he was subjected to questions like if anyone taught his daughters to hate Jews or whether by the "...very fact of being Muslim, you are not filling children, or those in the mosque, with hatefulness?" Sheila Jackson Lee (D-TX).[13] How was this happening? Why was this happening? Why must this bereaved man defend his faith when the subject of the hearing was a white nationalist? The dehumanization process continued and is still present.

On the Monday after the Christchurch shooting, one of my closest friends from high school, who was also my college roommate and became the principal of the Islamic high school we attended, texted our group of friends: "I'm meeting with kids all day, and I'm struggling. They are scared, sad, disgusted, and feeling helpless. This is tough." We could point her to mental health resources all day and night, but that would not take away from the reality of the situation. Why do Muslims need to be directed to therapy for a heinous crime that someone else committed? Is that fair? I thought that by the time 9/11 happened, I was already in medical school, my identity was already pretty set, and I was confident in who I was and what my religion represented.

Of course, today, I worry for my children on many levels. There are everyday mom things: Will they be happy and healthy? Will they fare well in school? Will they be able to get good jobs in the future? Will they be able to find a spouse who can also be their best friend?

Then, there are the Muslim mom things: Will they be a target of an Islamophobic attack? Will they suffer from an Islamophobic slur or hate crime? Will their faith be shaken by what they read or hear in the media as opposed to what they see in their everyday interactions with Muslims?

One day, sitting around the dinner table, we asked each child to talk about one fun thing they did at school that day. My 10-year-old, Hamza, spoke about playing flag football outside with his friends.

"Does officer K go outside with you guys during recess?" Amjad asked. I shot him a knowing glance. I was sad that he needed to ask that question but relieved that the answer was "Yes."

After Christchurch, Amjad announced one day, "I am going to go to shooter training, obtain a license to conceal and carry, and buy a gun."

"Over my dead body!" I retorted.

"Why over your dead body? We cannot just sit like lame ducks waiting for the next white supremacist to shoot us up!"

"The wild, wild west isn't the answer."

"Then, what is? Muslims should join the NRA. This country may have stricter gun control laws if masses of Muslims join the NRA."

"That's fine. You can join whatever you want, but I am not allowing a gun in our home with four kids."

My husband did not know I had spent years as a pediatric resident counseling families against keeping guns in the home. The AAP (American Academy of Pediatrics) spearheaded the ASK (Asking Saves Kids) campaign, which encouraged physicians to tell parents to ask about unlocked guns in the home before sending their children for a playdate. The AAP advocated that the safest home for a child was without a gun, but if a gun must be at home, it should be stored separately from the locked-up ammunition. It seemed that a gun locked away from its ammunition would not serve the purpose my husband was trying to achieve. For now, I keep winning this debate in our home.

I realized later that I could not blame Amjad for thinking that way. A month later, I flew to Atlanta to attend a medical conference. I spent the day after the meeting seeing some of Atlanta's most beautiful state parks. I returned to the city several hours earlier than my flight home. I tried to get in touch with a former roommate of mine, Angela, who was living in Atlanta at the time. Angela is Black, and her family has been in the US for generations. She is a former military officer. I told her about my adventures outside of Atlanta and how I wanted to hike around Stone Mountain. However, I saw the "Beware of Bears" sign and hesitated since I was alone.

"You should have told me you were here," she said. "I would have come with you for the hike and brought my gun."

"What? Come on, Angela, do you need a gun to shoot a bear?"

"The gun wouldn't be for the bear. The surrounding areas of Georgia are filled with white nationalist racists. It would have been to protect a hijab-wearing woman like you from the racists!"

Oh.

Knowing what I know today, I no longer need to defend my religion or apologize on behalf of someone who claims to share my tenets of faith because he decides to shoot up a nightclub. I don't hear of any right-wing extremist (politician or follower) apologizing on behalf of all their mistakes. According to a 2015 Pew research study, Muslims comprise 1.8 billion of the world's population.[14] Logic dictates that if 1.8 billion people adhered to a violent religion, the world would have been annihilated by now.

I want to share a little secret with you. I have spent the last 40+ years of my life interacting with Muslims and learning from all types of Muslims in all settings, whether in the mosque, parochial high school, or religious retreats. Not once was I taught to hate or kill anyone. I know, shocking, isn't it?!

I have been taught repeatedly that we, human beings, will be judged for our actions by a Just yet Merciful Lord. Our last efforts will supersede things we did when we were younger (perhaps not as refined). We are consistently taught not only to love another human being but that our faith is not complete until we love for our brothers [in humanity] what we love for ourselves. *Sound familiar?*

Another Islamic teaching is that we don't know about the final days of other human beings or our own. It isn't for us to judge or hate. Of course, that is nice, in theory. However, it is complex in practicality to hold back from being angry and judgmental regarding people who have hurt you individually or communally. Ultimately, so many of my co-religionists, fellow refugees, immigrants, migrants, and I believe that love trumps hate.

CHAPTER TWENTY

The Resistance

Over the last few years, since the campaign of then-candidate, Trump, and his subsequent presidency, the hateful anti-Muslim rhetoric has continued to rise. At the end of January 2017, I arranged to attend a pediatric medical conference hosted by the Cleveland Clinic in Dubai. My eldest son, Hamza, was eight years old and obsessed with buildings, Legos, and architecture. Day and night, he talked about wanting to see Burj Khalifa, as it was the tallest building on the planet. Amjad and I decided we would all go together. We surprised the children with this trip and captured the moment we told them about it on video. They jumped up and down with excitement. We were there for just over a week. While we were there, newly inaugurated President Trump signed an Executive Order for the first travel ban, preventing foreign nationals from seven predominantly Muslim countries, including Syria, from visiting the country for 90 days. How awful, I thought to myself, but I had resolved to try to enjoy the time with my family in Dubai.

Within the next 24-48 hours of the Executive Order, my Facebook account was filled with stories of people having difficulty coming back into the country. One story made me nervous: an American citizen of Syrian origin who was naturalized was denied re-entry. That was like me. A naturalized American citizen of Syrian origin! That night, after the kids had gone to sleep, I sat down to have a serious conversation with my husband.

"So, what will we do if I am denied re-entry?" I questioned Amjad, wide-eyed.

"That's not gonna happen," said Mr. Always Optimistic.

"How do you know that? It just happened to this other person."

"Well, it's not going to happen to you."

"You don't know that, and I will not get caught without a plan B! We have to have a plan B." As a doctor, I always make a plan B for when and if my patients decompensate.

He texted his friend, Ahmed Rehab, the director of the Chicago chapter of the Council on American-Islamic Relations, CAIR, a civil rights organization that had been actively involved in getting lawyers to help secure entry for people who were affected by the ban. He reassured my husband that he would help if I had any issues. Why did I have to think about a plan B for my future? Where could I practice medicine outside of the US? What country could we immigrate to that would be easy for our family to integrate into and learn the language of? The answer was "None." We did not know any other country. The United States was where our families and friends were. It was where we spent our childhood. It was where we knew the ins and outs, intricacies, and cultural details down to the most minute detail.

There is a fable circulating about putting frogs in boiling water. The legend says that if one puts a frog in tepid water and progressively makes the water hotter, the frog would not perceive the danger and would subsequently be boiled to death. That fable has since been debunked, but it does give something to think about. Is this phenomenon happening to the Muslim community in the U.S.? I wondered. The water is getting hotter and hotter, yet, we are expected not to react. We cannot get angry about the injustices we are facing because terrorists are just angry, and in being angry, we are just perpetuating the stereotype about us. But anyone else in this position would get mad. How much injustice does a community need to endure before reaching the boiling point?

In April 2018, President Trump tweeted a snippet of a talk that Minnesota Congresswoman Ilhan Omar gave interspersed with images of the twin towers burning on 9/11, taking her words out of context and titling his tweet 'WE WILL NEVER FORGET!" The video was viewed over 7 million times. With that tweet, he painted a big red target on her back and the backs of every other readily-identifiable Muslim, myself included. After 9/11, some Muslim scholars came out with a religious dispensation saying that Muslim women who feared for their lives should not wear the hijab in public. Not everyone agreed with this dispensation, but some women removed their head covering.

Many people see the hijab as a form of oppression. They cannot possibly understand why a woman would choose such for herself. The head covering has been a historical part of all three Abrahamic religious traditions. I have lived in the US practically my whole life. I work for a Catholic institution where many statues and pictures of the Virgin Mary, the mother of Jesus, are displayed. I have never seen the Virgin Mary depicted without her head covered at my workplace or any church across the country.

Moreover, the #MeToo movement was based on women loudly proclaiming that men did not have the right to touch women however they wanted. Men should not speak to women however they wanted to; women had autonomy over their bodies, and the time was up for unwelcomed gestures and commentary. Hijab takes that up a notch. Hijab gives women complete independence on who sees them in their private persona versus their public persona.

I never second-guessed wearing hijab until the year Donald Trump ran for president and during his term in office. I am by no means a coward or particularly risk-averse. I used to walk home from the library at the university at two in the morning every day. Hyde Park is not the safest neighborhood in the world. In medical school, I lived in a building with a bullet hole in the front entrance window. I recently traveled to a war zone while I was pregnant!

Nevertheless, I have never felt as threatened as I did in the year before and leading up to the Trump presidency. During those years, I had a heightened awareness of my surroundings. I took Krav Maga classes to defend myself should the need arise. I would turn around often after passing someone by to ensure they would not turn around and attack me. That never happened to me before the Trump presidency!

My faith, Islam, puts my physical safety as my top priority. I do not believe this is disputed amongst any Muslim scholar. And there are the naysayers in my community who say that we live in a diverse city and that I should not feel threatened. That I should stay strong and not think about removing my hijab. No one can tell me how I feel. No one can say to me that I should not or do not feel threatened. I am within my religious right to remove my hijab if I feel threatened. This is one of the many facets that I love about my faith. It is my direct and intimate relationship with God. God will judge my actions with the complete knowledge of all my circumstances, past and present, including my childhood, upbringing, education, experiences, and intentions.

Indeed, I believe wearing the hijab is a spiritual act of devotion to my Creator. Every day, before I leave my home, I get to decide to fulfill that act of faith. But I also believe that not wearing the hijab in an attempt to protect my life would also be an act of devotion. Only God is in a place to judge. For days and nights, I thought deeply about where I was in place and time and how the way I dressed would affect me and my family, mainly since I was usually out with my young children.

My last child, whom I carried through my trip to Yemen, Kareem, was quite colicky for the first six months of his life. A couple of months after his birth, I drove home with him in an unfamiliar neighborhood. Kareem was crying his head off non-stop, but I knew it was just colic. He was fed, changed, and burped before I left. I was driving faster than the speed limit to get home. I got pulled over by a police officer, an older white man. As soon as he walked up, I rolled down my window, and he heard my baby screaming his lungs out. He asked me if everything was okay.

"Yeah, he has colic. Thanks." After he told me I was speeding, I gave him my license, registration, and insurance card. He went back to the patrol car to run my license.

Kareem kept screaming his head off, so at some point, I just got out of the car and opened the back door to get him out to see if taking him out of the car seat would console him.

I got out of my car without thinking. Without worrying.

Later, after I got home, I relayed the story to Amjad.

"I didn't even think twice about it," I said. "I bet if I were a woman of color, I would have hesitated or maybe let my baby just cry rather than risk getting shot by getting out of the car while pulled over."

He shook his head in agreement.

Not only do I live in one of the most racially segregated cities in the US, but this city also saw the indictment and sentencing of a former Chicago Police officer, Jason Van Dyke, for shooting a 17-year-old young African-American man, LaQuan McDonald, 16 times. Also, I live in a country where African-American women are three to four times more likely to die than white mothers. African-American babies die at twice the rate of white babies. I know we have to do better. I have to do better.

Ultimately, I decided to keep my hijab on because I believed standing up against oppression and injustice is among the highest callings. It outweighed my individualized protection of myself and my children. My children, my husband, and I all had close friends from people of color or other marginalized groups. In solidarity with my fellow brothers and sisters in humanity, who will continue to feel threatened in the current political climate in our country and abroad, I resist white nationalism in every way, shape, and form possible.

CHAPTER TWENTY-ONE

The Building Blocks

I do see signs of change on the horizon. For example, support is building for Congresswoman Ilhan Omar, who refuses to back down. Support is building for her and the three other women of color members of Congress, whom former President Trump suggested should go back to their own countries despite all four being American citizens. Muslims are being more recognized as part and parcel of the fabric of this country. Ibtihaj Muhammad was recognized as the first hijab-wearing Muslim woman to represent the US in the Olympics as a fencer. She won a bronze medal. Major brands have started catering to the Muslim community. Nike designed a hijab for Muslim athletes. Macy's launched a collection by a Muslim designer producing modest clothing. Gap's most recent back-to-school campaign featured a girl in a hijab. Coca-Cola aired an ad highlighting the Ramadan fast. Representation matters, and the fact that my children (and other American children) can see images of Muslims in mainstream culture, has helped.

Medelita, a medical apparel company, recently launched a hijab for Muslim doctors. The month before I started medical school, I did not know any Muslim-American women who were doctors. My sister was hanging out with me in my bedroom as I was trying to figure out how I would put a stethoscope on with my hijab on. Would I have to untie my hijab to put the stethoscope on? Or should I put it on top of my hijab and directly into my ears? I tried several different ways, with my sister giving me suggestions. I got so frustrated by the end. "The patient will die before I get my stethoscope on!" Now there is a hijab explicitly designed to use a stethoscope.

Many of my fellow Americans are outright disgusted by how

migrants and refugees have been treated at the border. Physician organizations like the American Academy of Pediatrics and the Infectious Diseases Society of America, made statements criticizing how our government was treating the migrants who were trying to cross our southern border to seek asylum. Charitable organizations made up of average fellow citizens were trying to figure out ways to help these people. Lawyers were helping them know their legal rights and aiding with their paperwork. These people have given me hope and reassured me that the light of humanity could never be extinguished.

However, I read things that keep my sense of awareness heightened, like a report by Genocide Watch that describes the stages of genocide, "It starts when demagogic leaders define a target group as 'the other' and claim it is a threat to the interests of supporters."[15] Discrimination follows, and members of the out-group are deemed subhuman. Genocides flourish when their architects chip away at the in-group's empathy for the out-group. The "you-are-with-us-or-against-us" phase follows.

The report continued by highlighting how many perpetrators of massacres are not remorseful because they rationalize the murders. Genocide scholar, James Waller, interviewed dozens of Hutu men responsible for the atrocities committed against the Tutsis, some even committing heinous acts of violence against children. "Their rationale, according to Waller, was: 'If I didn't do this, those children would have grown up to come back to kill me. This was something that was a necessity for my people to be safe, for my people to survive.'"[15]

But just as there was hope for Adam, the Syrian refugee who was resettled in Germany, the work of German neuroscientist, Tania Singer, has demonstrated that there is hope for others; that perhaps people can be trained in compassion.

"Singer's group has shown that subjects trained in this form of loving-kindness meditation had a more compassionate response—as measured by the activation of certain brain circuits—than untrained subjects, when watching short film clips of people in pain."[15]

Every year, the night before my children start a new school year, I sit them down and read a blog on *Momastery* entitled "The Talk."[16] It is a letter from a mom to her new third-grader telling him about a time when she was in grade school and knew a little boy named Adam, who was being excluded. However, she did not do anything about it. And how she regrets that. She tries to teach her son always to remember to be kind and that being kind is more important than bringing home good grades. Every night, before my children go to bed, I ask them to name an act of kindness they did that day. I did not know about Singer's studies before I started these two traditions in my family, but I agree that teaching empathy and fostering compassion needs to start early.

I think about empathy a lot and what it means. The Merriam-Webster definition of "empathy" is the feeling that one understands and shares another person's experiences and emotions. I believe empathy lies on a continuum. On one end of the spectrum lies empathy and secondary trauma, while on the other end lies hatred to the degree of dehumanization, allowing for dispensability. My local NPR (National Public Radio) station aired a segment on the downfall of too much empathy. Author Fritz Breithaupt was interviewed on his forthcoming book, "The Dark Sides of Empathy." He talked about one of the downfalls of too much empathy: it can spark violence. Breithaupt argues that when someone empathizes and takes another's side, they become blinded to all other perspectives, and "that empathy can fuel seeing the other side as darker and darker or more dubious."[17]

I can see that. Too much empathy can make you blind to the other side. And that is what extremists want us to do. To be so blind to one side or the other that we can never see a person on the other side changing. The older I get, the more life experiences I have, and the more I see the wisdom behind always leaving the door open. No matter how someone is today, it does not mean that tomorrow's life circumstances will prevent them from doing a complete 180.

Scientists tell us that humans are all the same down to the smallest building blocks. No one knows that more than a doctor or a scientist who has studied genetics and cellular biology—the identical four nucleotides paired together by hydrogen bonds. Everyone has the same ones: Adenine, Thymine, Guanine, and Cytosine. On a more macro level, when a patient is lying open on the OR (operating room) table, with his head screened off from his body as is typical in surgery, the surgeon cannot tell if the patient is black, white, Asian, Christian, Muslim, Jewish, Hindu, or atheist. I can tell you that first-hand from rotating through surgery as a medical student. The organs are indistinguishable among races, ethnicities, and religions. What exacerbates the apparent differences if our building blocks are the same?

CHAPTER TWENTY-TWO

Just One

Just as a surgeon cannot distinguish the race, ethnicity, or religion of the patient lying open beneath their scalpel, other entities cannot do so either—entities like viruses. A virus does not ask you about your background or your faith. As we learned in 2020, a virus does not even ask you or care if you believe in its existence. How many people died in the last few years who thought COVID-19 was a hoax?

In early 2020, when the pandemic hit the United States, I had been a practicing physician for 17 years. On a chilly January morning, I headed to work thinking things would be business as usual, but nothing was further from the truth. When I parked my car, I could not miss the multiple police cars parked in the lot. When I entered the hospital wearing my gray lab coat and physician ID badge, I knew something was wrong when security officers greeted me. *Maybe a patient has absconded, or a family member was getting violent.*

When I finally got to the pediatric floor, everything looked the same, so I got down to business, looking up patients' lab results, overnight vitals, and chest X-rays or CT scans. I asked the nurses about our common patients. Finally, I ran into the charge nurse.

"Why is there so much security downstairs and outside? What's going on?"

She got close to me and whispered. "The adult side admitted a patient with the new coronavirus."

The day I had predicted had arrived. My hospital had admitted the second American patient with the novel coronavirus, and I knew it was just a matter of time before there would be thousands of others. In January 2020, the virus had not even been officially named, nor had the World Health Organization (WHO) declared a pandemic. Yet, by this time, I had spent more than 20 hours researching and writing a manual for healthcare workers in the Middle East and North African regions on how to deal with patients infected with this new virus on behalf of MedGlobal.

I read everything our Chinese colleagues had reported to the WHO. I learned about the clinical manifestation, infectivity (R_0), incubation period, and death rate. The most problematic aspect was the contagiousness of the virus and the long incubation period. A long incubation period with high contagiousness meant a patient who did not know they were infected would infect many others before they knew their diagnosis.

Soon after I completed the manual, my hospital held a press conference announcing the admission of the second American COVID-19 patient and, soon after that, her husband. Friends and family who saw the news were texting me, asking me if I was safe. Even though I worked on the women and children's side of the hospital, I frequented the adult side because it housed the cafeteria, a coffee stand, and the multi-faith room where I prayed.

I spent most of February 2020 fighting with members of the department of public health to get some of my patients tested for COVID. The Department restricted testing to patients who had traveled or had an epidemiological link to a traveler or a known infected person.

"Come on! This virus is here on US soil. This is ridiculous. Why are you restricting my access to testing? This girl is five years old; she has bilateral pneumonia of unknown origin, is not responding to antibiotics, is viral panel negative, and is extremely sick. She deserves to be tested. You can't tell me that the first few adults admitted to American hospitals didn't infect others on the airplane."

I felt sorry for the public health officials. They were overwhelmed and did not have enough test reagents or kits. I was thankful they eventually listened to me when I called.

I spent most of the following month reading and following the news. I knew that a group of families who attended my local mosque and my kids' school were planning to travel to Mecca for the *umrah*, the Lesser Pilgrimage for Spring Break. I anticipated that the trip would be a disaster waiting to happen because either the families would get sick in Mecca or bring the virus home to our community and school.

I tried to convince the president of the mosque and the *imam* to cancel. However, I felt like Chicken Little. I was screaming. "The sky is falling!" But no one else saw it.

It was time for Plan B.

I headed to social media and posted on February 29, 2020:

There is a false sense of security that COVID-19 is not rampant in the US. That is because we are not testing enough.

There have been [three] new cases (one in California, one in Oregon, and one in Washington state) with no epidemiologic connection. That means it is in the community.

In weeks, the US will likely have hundreds of cases. It would be irresponsible of the KSA [government] to keep *umrah* open for Americans especially given the nature of *umrah* with people being up close and personal due to crowding.

It would be irresponsible of Americans to go.

That was my expert opinion, and I only shared it because one day, I will answer God about what I did with that knowledge.

What's Plan C? I knew a Saudi urban planner who had connections to the Saudi government. I planned to email him and say the same thing. Indeed, he would have been well aware of one of the many *hadiths*, sayings of the Prophet Muhammad (peace be upon him), addressing plagues. The one I would have referred him to was: "When you hear that a plague is in a land, do not go to it, and if it occurs in a land that you are already in, then do not leave it." Thankfully soon after that, on March 4th, the Saudi government banned all *umrah* visitors from coming into their country.

One week after the *umrah* ban, the WHO officially declared that SARS-CoV2 had moved to pandemic status. Two days after that, our government declared a state of national emergency. I spent so much time in March 2020 on social media. I did Facebook Lives and webinars to educate the public about what was happening. I tried to balance between warning people to take public health instructions seriously and not paralyzing them with fear. My posts were always meant for the public, regardless of religion. I never viewed the pandemic as a strictly Muslim issue; instead, I considered my responsibilities toward humanity through the lens of my faith. I was firmly bound by the *hadith* of the parable of the ship that would get destroyed if the people on the upper deck did not prevent the people from the lower deck from making a hole in the vessel to get water.

In March 2020, the boards of mosques across the county were contemplating whether or not to close the mosques. The board of my local mosque asked me to join their next meeting. I went head-to-head with an ER physician, letting board members know why I thought it was imperative that the mosque close for the five daily congregational prayers and the Friday prayer.

Because people stand shoulder-to-shoulder in the prayers and many of the attendees of the congregational prayers were older, I argued that holding the communal prayers would be putting people in harm's way. I cited another *hadith*, "There should be neither harming nor reciprocation of harm." The *imam* backed me up, but some board members were swayed by the ER doctor's opinion against closure. Ultimately, the local health department shut all religious institutions down.

In April 2020, I was consulted on a previously healthy six-year-old patient admitted to the pediatric intensive care unit for heart failure. I was convinced that he must have had COVID-19, even though he tested negative.

"Test him again," I asked the pediatric intensivist.

"Nour, we sent the test off again. It's pending, but it's going to take another day. Maybe it's not COVID-19." Kelly, the intensivist, said.

"I am not so sure. Let's get a CT scan. Maybe, he has bilateral ground glass infiltrates. That would be enough for me."

She put in the stat order. The radiology tech calls the PICU five minutes later.

"Dr. Akhras, they won't take him until his COVID test comes back," Samantha, the ICU nurse informed me.

"Seriously?!"

"They are on hold. You want to talk to them?" Samantha offered.

"Sure. I will."

I got on the phone and asked to speak to the radiologist.

"What do you mean you can't scan him without the test result?" I asked him.

"Well, the cleaning protocol is extensive if he is positive, so we just need to know," he replied.

"Listen, this virus is here to stay. It's not going anywhere. And this is a hospital. We need to do tests regardless of a patient's COVID status." I proceeded.

Silence followed as he was not convinced. Yet.

"This CT scan is going to change my management. This kid is in heart failure. I need to know whether he has ground glass opacities," I pressed on.

Thank God, he finally agreed to take him down.

He tested negative for COVID again. I tried different treatment modalities on him until one worked, and he was finally discharged from the hospital six days later. I did not know then that this patient's clinical status was due to COVID, but not acute COVID. He had what the CDC eventually named MIS-C (multi-system inflammatory syndrome in children). Two weeks after he was discharged, pediatric physicians across the United Kingdom reported an entity named PIMS (Paediatric Multi-System Inflammatory Syndrome temporarily associated with

SARS-CoV2). I read everything I could get my hands on about this disease entity. Then, I started teaching physician colleagues stateside about everything I learned from managing my patient and what I learned from my European colleagues.

For all the backlash Muslims had received over the last two decades, I was confident that American-Muslim physicians (many immigrants or refugees or their children) like myself, had done their due diligence and gone above and beyond in treating our patients. We developed isolation protocols, diagnostic and treatment protocols, and vaccination protocols to deal with a newly emerging pathogen. While members of the Trump administration had invested so much in vilifying people like me, we worked unwaveringly to protect the public's health, even while the President himself was leading the most extraordinary misinformation campaign as he downplayed the effects of COVID-19. The irony should not be lost on emerging right-wing politicians anywhere in the world that the leading scientists who discovered the first vaccine against COVID-19 were two Turkish Muslim immigrants to Germany, Dr. Ugur Sahin and Dr. Ozlem Tureci.

To say that 2020 was a challenging year would be the understatement of the century. As an American physician, I was reusing personal protective equipment to evaluate COVID-19 patients. I was battling misinformation in the American public, some from the Muslim community. I was trying my best to protect my family, including my four little children, from being infected with COVID-19 while trying to protect their mental health. I was acutely aware of the spike in mental health crises affecting children because of school and societal shutdowns. Our hospital's number of pediatric admissions due to mental health issues, had skyrocketed. It seemed that these were the only pediatric patients being admitted.

In December 2020, when I became one of the first Americans eligible for the COVID-19 vaccine, I was ecstatic. Don't get me wrong. I was also apprehensive. After all, there was no long-term data. Also, I had a previous history of anaphylaxis from an injectable medication. I was worried about that aspect as well. I read all the studies and looked at the data. As my habit, I prayed the *istikhara* prayer and signed up.

On vaccine day, I packed a bag in case I ended up in the ER and needed admission. I prayed for ease, rolled up my sleeve with some friends, and received my first vaccine in mid-December. I was overwhelmed with relief that I tolerated the vaccine well. And three weeks later, I received my second dose.

I updated my social media pages periodically with new and pertinent information. I tried to make informed decisions balancing risks and benefits. I kept reading to keep updated on the latest data on medication for children. I fielded calls from friends, family, and people I did not know about exposure scenarios, how long people should be isolated, if they should test, cancel trips, plan weddings, etc. I fielded questions from my newly-pregnant colleagues during a pandemic with a new pathogen. I answered questions from the administrations of some Islamic schools (grade schools, high schools, and religious seminaries) across the country.

When the vaccines rolled out for children, I participated in another round of Facebook lives, educational sessions, and international news agency interviews. The Department of Health and Human Services of the White House facilitated the most surprising session I participated in. I forwarded the email sent out by the White House that detailed that session with my name and credentials to my mom and dad. "I have come a long way from the FBI's most wanted list!" I had joked.

In the summer of 2022, a little over two years into the pandemic, I got a phone call from a physician who was a mutual friend of mine and Amjad's, who also happened to run in Muslim leadership circles.

"Thank you for everything you have done to protect the community from COVID-19." He started.

"Oh. Um. Thanks."

"You know, to be honest, I did not believe all the hype at first either. I also thought you were crazy." He continued.

"Uh-huh."

"But it turns out you were right. And I appreciate everything you did." He proceeded.

"Yeah. No problem."

"I hope you weren't negatively affected by what people said about you."

"Excuse me?" I did not understand what he was saying.

"I mean, how people talked about you."

I remained silent.

"Did you not even know what they said?" He asked.

"No, not really. When you have four kids and a full-time job, there is little time for much else."

"Oh. Well, that's good, I guess."

"Yeah."

"I am glad you didn't hear or read that stuff," he concluded.

I did not ask for names or details, and he did not offer any.

After we hung up, I reflected on what he had said. Some were vilifying me in my community for my strong stances regarding the virus. Perhaps that should have made me sad. But instead, I again reflected on the verse in the Qur'an that is so central to everything I do.

"Whoever saves one life, it is as if he has saved all of humanity."

Any effort I had exerted to prevent someone from getting infected or super sick with COVID-19 or dying from COVID, if it helped save one life, it was worth all of it. The time, the energy, the sleepless nights, the defamation, all of it. And the same for becoming a physician: all the minutes spent studying, reading, memorizing, making flashcards, the hours spent in the anatomy lab, if it helped save one life. The same goes for medical missions: the fear, the missing my children, the food poisoning, the secondary trauma; if it saved one life, it was all worth it.

Why does the verse specify one life? Just one life. Just one.

Is it because it only takes one human being to change the traje of humanity? If we think about modern history: Ernest Fleming, Marie Curie, Albert Einstein, Anne Frank, Rosa Parks, and Steve Jobs, among others, come to mind. These individuals were just one person whose contribution(s) significantly affected the rest of humanity.

However, isn't that one of the paradoxes of the human condition? That even though one person can have a profound effect on the rest of us, we know as human beings that no one did it alone. Every one of us had people raising, teaching, supporting, comforting, and encouraging us.

Still, that Quranic verse taught me never to underestimate our contributions to just one person's life. In other words, you may be just one person, but your contribution to that person's life could be exactly what they needed to change the trajectory of humanity for good.

So be that one person. Don't underestimate anyone's potential. Open your heart and mind to people, even or *especially* to refugees. Maybe one of them will be that person who affects the rest of the world. After all, we know that sometimes, it takes only one person to affect humanity positively. Just one.

Acknowledgements

I shouldn't be here today. I mean, I should not even be alive because at the age of three, I was in the living room of our family home in Homs, Syria, and picked up a water bottle that was near the old kerosene heater used to keep the home warm. The clear liquid inside must have looked like water to my 3-year-old self, but in fact, it was the kerosene that my grandfather stored in the bottle. I aspirated it into my lungs, giving me chemical aspiration pneumonia. Had it not been for my father's quick thinking, I don't know what would have happened. He decided to drive me to a hospital in the capital city, nearly 2 hours away, and treat me for the duration, in our home, with intravenous antibiotics. This was at a time long before home health care and peripherally-inserted central catheters were ever invented. Honestly, I probably would have died. It goes without saying that this was not the first or last time my dad's medical knowledge helped me.

I shouldn't have become a doctor, either. In my third year of medical school, I had adamantly decided that I was done. I was quitting, and no one was going to get in the way of me extricating myself from the miserable existence of being a medical student. It was my mother who saw how close I was to the finishing line and recruited my sister, who lived across the globe at the time, to encourage me until I agreed to "just get the degree."

I am only who I am today because of the unwavering support of these three individuals. And to them, I will be eternally indebted.

This project was born after what seemed to me a chance encounter between the author, Dave Eggers, and me, along with the subject of one of his books, *The Monk of Mocha*, Mokhtar al-Khanshali, when they visited Chicago during a book tour. During that encounter, the power of storytelling came into clear focus.

So in March 2019, after a conversation with my husband, Amjad, I felt motivated to start writing. I will never forget telling him, "There's no way I could ever write a book. I don't have enough to say. Maybe it will just be an essay." Then, I started writing and writing and writing. Never in my wildest dreams did I think this would turn into a book.

During so many hurdles along the way, I hesitated, intended to walk away, and thought to myself: *This is stupid!* But Amjad would not let me give up. "You already wrote it." He would keep reminding me. Thus, this book would not have launched without him.

Countless other people were instrumental in my journey to becoming an author. Too many friends to enumerate here who cheered me on whenever I mentioned the thought of writing a book. Thank you to my former roommate, Amenah Ibrahim, for always having my back and ultimately connecting me to my publisher, Janan Sarwar. I could not have done this without Janan's infectious energy, warmth, encouragement, and unwavering support. My initial set of readers: Karen Fernandez, John Kahler, Carol Lambert Akhras, Aminah Salah, and Khadija Ahmed provided vital constructive criticism and guidance. I am appreciative of the instrumental feedback I received from Feryal Salem and Haaris Ahmad.

Initial editorial remarks from John Hanc and Martha Murphy lead to subsequent steps. But if you really want to experience an ego-shattering phenomenon, hand what you think is your best work to an unbiased, excellent editor like Rumki Chowdhury. She helped polish up all of the rough edges. I am also deeply humbled by the suggestions and advice of journalist Lauren Wolfe.

The beautiful aesthetics of this book are attributed to my ultra-talented friends, Hanane Korchi and Sumaiyya Rahman. I am grateful to my friend Tammie Ismail who introduced me to my brilliant photographer, Alana Marcelle-Hendricks. Alana braved the fierce cold of Chicago to capture eye-pleasing images. I am also thankful for the UNHCR (United Nations High Commissioner for Refugees) Media team for allowing me to use the front image as my cover.

I can't underestimate the power of encouragement by women who I met along the way like Cathy Humikowski and Loretta Poisson. And I would be remiss to not mention my English teacher from junior high and high school, Mrs. Roberta Gates, who is easily the first identifiable person in my memory who strengthened and helped refine my writing skills.

At the front of this list, of course, is God. It sounds almost cliche to say that I am thankful to God for everything. However, nothing could be more accurate than that. I have easily seen the Hand of God in every single step in this endeavor. From (what I thought were) chance meetings with people over 20 years ago, to happening to be at the right time and the right place, to everything occurring at the perfect time. Even through the multiple rejection letters I received through this undertaking. Not to mention the very fact of my existence, my health, my ability to think, see, use my hands to type, and every other blessing God is responsible for that we are completely oblivious to. If nothing else, I pray that God continues to provide me with health and ability to help people as long as I breathe the air of this planet.

REFERENCES

1. Rotella, Sebastian. "Global Right-Wing Extremism Networks Are Growing, the U.S. Is Just Now Catching up. *ProPublica*, 22 Jan 2021, https://www.propublica.org/article/global-right-wing-extremism-networks-are-growing-the-u-s-is-just-now-catching-up.

2. Britannica, The Editors of Encyclopaedia. "Arab Spring." *Encyclopedia Britannica*, 23 Nov. 2022, https://www.britannica.com/event/Arab-Spring. Edited 25 November 2022.

3. Amos, Deborah. "30 Years Later, Photos Emerge from Killings in Syria." *NPR*, NPR, 2 Feb 2012, https://www.npr.org/2012/02/01/146235292/30-years-later-photos-emerge-from-killings-in-syria.

4. "Speech at the Academy of Motion Picture Arts and Sciences Governors Awards, 2013." *Lapham's Quarterly*, Conversations. https://www.laphamsquarterly.org/conversations/bernard-mandeville-angelina-jolie

5. "Yemen Conflict Explained in 400 Words." *BBC News*, BBC, 13 June 2018, https://www.bbc.com/news/world-middle-east-44466574.

6. Almosawa, Shuaib, et al. "'It's a Slow Death': The World's Worst Humanitarian Crisis." *The New York Times*, The New York Times, 23 Aug 2017, www.nytimes.com/interactive/2017/08/23/world/middleeast/yemen-cholera-humanitarian-crisis.html.

7. Pagan, Camille Noe. "When Doctors Downplay Women's Health Concerns." *The New York Times*, The New York Times, 3 May 2018, https://www.nytimes.com/2018/05/03/well/live/when-doctors-downplay-womens-health-concerns.html.

8. Service, Mail Foreign. "'I Didn't Think of Iraqis as Humans,' Says U.S. Soldier Who Raped 14-Year-Old Girl before Killing Her and Her Family." *Daily Mail Online*, Associated Newspapers, 21 Dec. 2010, https://www.dailymail.co.uk/news/article-1340207/I-didnt-think-Iraqis-humans-says-U-S-soldier-raped-14-year-old-girl-killing-her-family.html.

9. Clark, Simon, et al. "American Has Exported Hater. After the New Zealand attacks, it must rein it in | View." *Euronews*, 18 Mar. 2019, https://www.euronews.com/2019/03/16/new-zealand-shooting-was-inspired-hate-america-exporting-we-need-ncna983936.

10. "Funding Fear of Muslims: $206M Went to Promoting 'Hatred', Report Finds." *The Guardian*, Guardian News and Media, 20 June 2016, https://www.theguardian.com/us-news/2016/jun/20/islamophobia-funding-cair-berkeley-report.

11. "Researcher: Disparities Exist in News Coverage of Terror Attacks." *University of Alabama News*, https://news.ua.edu/2019/02/researcher-disparities-

exist-in- news-coverage-of-terror-attacks/.

12. "Terror Attacks by Muslims Receive 357% More Press Attention, Study Finds." *The Guardian*, Guardian News and Media, 20 July 2018, https://www.theguardian.com/us-news/2018/jul/20/muslim-terror-attacks-press-coverage-study.

13. Jindia, Shilpa. "Republicans Twist White Nationalism Hearing into Islamophobic Forum." *Truthout*, Truthout, 11 Apr. 2019, https://truthout.org/articles/republicans-twist-white-nationalism-hearing-into-islamophobic-forum/.

14. Lipka, Michael. "Muslims and Islam: Key Findings in the U.S. and around the World." *Pew Research Center*, Pew Research Center, 8 Dec 2020, https://www.pewresearch.org/fact-tank/2017/08/09/muslims-and-islam-key-findings-in-the-u-s-and-around-the-world/.

15. National Geographic. "What Science Tells Us about Good and Evil." *Genocidewatch*, Genocidewatch, 16 Aug 2017, https://www.genocidewatch.com/single-post/2017/08/16/what-science-tells-us-about-good-and-evil.

16. Doyle, Glennon. "The Talk." *Momastery*, 27 Mar. 2015, https://momastery.com/blog/2012/08/23/the-talk/.

17. Lamber, Jonathan. "Does Empathy Have a Dark Side?" *NPR*, NPR, 12 Apr. 2019, https://www.npr.org/sections/health-shots/2019/04/12/712682406/does-empathy-have-a-dark-side.

About the Author

Dr. Nour Akhras is a board-certified pediatric infectious diseases physician who has been working at a free-standing Women and Children's Hospital in the suburbs of Chicago for the last decade. Dr. Akhras was trained in pediatrics at the University of Illinois Chicago Medical Center and completed her fellowship at the University of Michigan, Ann Arbor. She holds a BA in Cellular and Molecular Biology from the University of Chicago and received her medical degree from Rush Medical College.

Dr. Akhras was trained in traditional Islamic sciences in Damascus, Syria, and has her *ijaza* in *tajwid* through the late Shaykh Hasan al-Kurdi. She has contributed a chapter on Islamic bioethics to a book published by Yale University entitled *What's the Point? Clinical Reflections on Care that Seems Futile*.

She has served on the board of IMAN (Inner City Muslim Action Network). This grassroots organization fosters transformational change in urban communities where she co-chaired IMAN's youth group, Pillars, for many years. She has also participated in multiple medical missions to support Syrian refugees in Hatay, Turkey, Thessaloniki, Greece, and displaced war victims in Ma'rib, Yemen. She has served on the boards of MedGlobal and the Syrian American Medical Society Midwest chapter. She has advocated for the rights of refugees by authoring op-eds in newspapers like *USA Today* and the *Chicago Sun-Times*. She has led speaking engagements, including presenting at Washington DC's National Press Club, discussing the effects of Syrian war violence on the lives of Syrian women.

She loves to travel, read, and swim in her free time. She takes bike rides and walks with her family and supports her children, who play basketball games. One may also find her attending gatherings with her sister, cousins, and high school friends.